The Germans
H John Grube

press twenty-one

ISBN 978-3-9817419-6-4

"We are (standing) on the eve of the possibility of a revolution in Europe"

"Wir stehen am Vorabend der Möglichkeit einer Revolution in Europa"

Helmut Schmidt
Chancellor of the Federal Republic of Germany1974 to 1982 on Phoenix TV - Die Zeit
Wirtschaftsforum; Monday 12 November 2012

For Randolph, Natascha and Philip
Rachel; Golo; Meike
Niklas and Alix; Jacob and Josephine

Contents

At First Glance

When it comes to expertise and knowledge bankers in recent years have lost their aura of infallibility. Their mantra was track record, looking at past performance and projecting the findings you derive there from into the future. But what are we to say about a country that since its inception as a nation state in 1871 has been the stage for two empires that failed catastrophically, each of them defaulting on incredibly huge sums of money, one lasting for forty-three (43) and the other for no more than twelve (12) years? With that kind of track record you will find it hard to get a car loan, not to mention a mortgage on your house. Why should we trust the Germans blind when we know that since about 1971 the Federal Republic of Germany has not been able to balance the books, running up a huge national debt to this day? And on top of it all: Germany started and lost two world wars in less than fifty years. This is not about scare mongering. It is about sharpening awareness.

We tend to subscribe to the assumption that history does not repeat itself but if it actually did the resemblances would be minor. Can we accept that as true? From history we know about the three Punic Wars, in which the Carthaginians of North Africa tried to defeat the Romans and conquer their empire. After losing wars Nos 1 and 2 the Carthaginians bounced back and had another go at the Romans. After war No 3, remembered for their bold and courageous commander Hannibal, famous for crossing the Alps with elephants, the Romans finished them off once and for all. Carthage became a desolate and deserted spot on the map and has remained so to this day.

The Germans have had their wars Nos 1 and 2, both with a disastrous outcome for the country and the world; and they bounced back. Will they be wise enough not to have another go, which might lead to No 3, the non-survivable one? At this moment hardly anybody sees any risk of a military conflict that would involve the Germans in a significant way, but what about a major conflict that erupts over socio-economic issues?

Already there are shouts of German hegemony, dominating the European economies. Euro-scepticism is on the rise, fuelling the re-birth of anti-German sentiment – if it actually ever did go away completely. After World War I German heavy industry and finance paved the way towards the next disaster. In the dying days of World War II some of Germany's economic might went under ground, escaping to South America or safe havens in Switzerland, to jump back on the scene when the time was right. There may be a stratum of German expatriate economic power that continues to work away from public attention and scrutiny. Could there be a powerful force, hidden from view and outside public accountability that is quietly pulling the strings and running the country through the back-door?

Having been trained as an engineer I like the word caution, going ahead in a circumspect way. I have written down some of my thoughts on the country and which way it appears to be going, based on personal experience and insights gained through having lived and survived through challenges, and - needless to add - it is not intended as a work of scholarly research.

Through a combination of having persevered and the passage of time I draw on a background of some forty years in the planning, development and implementation of multi-faceted international projects, where numerous elements interact and need to be forecast correctly, so as to tailor expenditure to the demands of cost-effectiveness. Whilst financiers are happy with extrapolating known trends observed in the past, planners need to recognise possible or likely deviations from steady growth scenarios. This has sharpened their problem awareness and anticipation. In our harsh reality political decision-makers tend to limit their scope to winning the next election, often leaving the planner in the un-enviable role of being the prophet that nobody wanted to listen to when there was still time. Hence there may be few if any people willing to help us look ahead.

Having had my fair share of that I have tried to preserve an unbiased outlook and good judgment. I like to think of myself as someone rather 'Mid-Atlantic', as some friendly soul might say. I have seen things happen, among them much that I did not like, that brought harmful and damaging effects. If in some small way being able to help avoiding the repetition of past mistakes lies within my limited powers, my rationale for writing a book about the Germans is to alert public awareness. They will be a decisive factor in times to come. We need to take them seriously, try to understand them and – if at all possible – anticipate how they will deal with things that may very well happen in their sphere of influence.

Rather than in a contiguous book that runs from start to finish I have chosen the form of presenting individual subjects in a number of episodes, loosely strung together, which in their entirety do not intend to present a complete picture - just the points about which I feel rather strongly. They reflect certain events or circumstances and my personal views and experience of them. This entails the risk that there are mild cases of repetition, as the episodes need to follow their own logic. Be patient and forgiving.

I survived the Nazis with their obscene Third Reich and World War II and was fortunate and privileged to make the best of what educational opportunities and an enlightened work atmosphere rendered possible after the end of all the horrors. I was able to soak up a bit of the American way of life, European culture, Britishness and French savoir vivre, with Immanuel Kant never quite out of sight.

My quest in writing this book is to help people gain an insight into how Germany and the Germans tick so that they may draw their own conclusions. Much of what we have come to learn about the recent past and the role that Germany played in it is hard to believe. This is an attempt to let us look at how all that came about.

Questions

Ever since its creation out of what was left of the failed Third Reich the Federal Republic of Germany or short Germany has been going from strength to strength. It doesn't really matter whether Germany ranks among the world's top ten economies, the top five or the top three. The emphasis is on the word top as opposed to somewhere in the middle or at the very bottom of the ladder. Germany is a force to be reckoned with.

But in recent times an atmosphere of unease has been surrounding Germany. This is arising from within the country as well as from without, suggesting that not all is perhaps as good as it could and should be. People are raising eyebrows, taking another look and asking questions. It is by no means a storm of protest, more like an undercurrent of critical interest. Anything stronger would seem out of proportion, like the suggestion that the country needs saving.

Going by what we have come to know about Germany we can relax, can't we? Germany continues to come across as the proverbial rock in the choppy seas of Europe and a multitude of nations has been making strenuous efforts to become a part of the European Union. But now the tide may be turning. Has the rise of Germany peaked, gone past the point at which we could file the country's rebirth as a job well done? Perhaps this is one of the better moments to say: wait a minute; let's see how good – or bad - it really is. Same as corporations from time to time need to reassess their situation, scope and objectives we may need to take stock and ask some basic questions:

- Is there a consensus in the estimation of most Germans that the country is going in the right direction?

- Conversely, does a significant number voice concern and ask for reappraisal of the country's fabric and fibre, to change or improve salient aspects?

- And what about the rest of the world; are they happy with the direction in which Germany is going?

At this moment the honest answer is perhaps at best a wholehearted I don't know. There are more questions than answers. One thing is certain: at present there is hardly anybody from among those whose opinion usually counts who thinks that the country is riding the crest of a wave. People are seeking answers and feel insecure about Germany's future.

Going back in recent history, spanning the period following World War II, one cannot but notice that Germany is far from being engulfed in that spirit of optimism that was characteristic for the late 1950s to early 1970s and the years of the Wirtschaftswunder, the at the time most amazing economic miracle, as it was referred to by many.

Looking at the history of the Federal Republic of Germany since then, these may be some of the questions to ask, not in any particular order but in the belief that they encompass the range of what challenges the country faces:

- What turned Germany from cash-rich into debt-ridden? Under the country's first chancellor Konrad Adenauer one of their greatest problems was to explain the so called Julius-Turm, literally Julius Tower, a German idiom for a slightly illicit treasure, a hoard of unallocated cash in government coffers above and beyond budget needs, which Adenauer and his economics sidekick had somehow stashed away. Wouldn't it be nice to have that problem today?

- What happened to the Soziale Marktwirtschaft, the social market economy, the state's implied if not outright declared commitment to fairness and social balance, emphasised on many a suitable occasion by – probably – every chancellor of the Federal Republic to this day?

- What is the quality of life experienced today by the majority of the country's inhabitants?

- Is the country under threat in its substance, its stated goals and aspirations and its ability to fulfil its obligations as prescribed by the country's constitution? We are not thinking of external threats but rather forces that arise out of the situation that has been allowed to establish itself within the country.

- If any of these questions require remedying, is it realistic to assume that in the light of political reality experienced to this day the appropriate constitutional bodies will be able to pass into law suitable legislation in good time?

- How probable is that? What if such an approach does not solve the problem? What options are there?

- Does the country need saving? If so, what or whom from? And a bit more rudely:

- Is the country – such as it is today - worth saving? Are there perhaps one or two things worth saving while the rest of it may need an overhaul?

But there is one question that outranks every other, given the fact that Germany was at the heart if not the outright instigator of the two most devastating wars in living human memory:

- Can it happen again? Is there anything inherent in the makeup of today's Germany that should give any cause for concern on that account?

Let us jump right into the middle of things, recapping some of the highlights: Germany has settled into living with a notorious budget deficit and a staggering national debt. As already mentioned its aggregate total has exceeded €2,000,000,000,000 with an upward tendency. I wrote out the numbers to avoid language confusion: a US 'billion' is a 'milliard' the German way. As at this time there exists absolutely no idea of how the country is *ever* going to repay this whilst the annual national budget continues to show a deficit.

There is considerable unemployment, masked in part by vast numbers of people being in so-called 'programs', working short time or in subsidised, low-income subsistence employment. Unemployment numbers have been improving but appearances are deceptive. Over the last few years there has been a shift in the quality of employment with a steady reduction of adequately paid jobs towards an increase in the low-pay segment, moving close to subsistence level income.

As soon as I wrote down my concerns I felt the need to put them into perspective. I have been increasingly haunted by the vision that I may be the only person to think that Germany is in a problem zone. Ask the man or woman in the street and they will all say it is even worse elsewhere, which translates into: nothing to worry about if you are a German, living in the country and looking at Germany.

But then consider this. Of the top eight economies only Japan and Russia fared worse, coming through the 2008/9 economic decline, with Germany's GDP having gone down by over six per cent, while that of the US dropped by around only half of that at a mere three, closely followed by France and the UK. This has not yet filtered through into public awareness in a country that quite openly and publicly has awarded itself two world championship titles: one for exports and the other for world travel. Phrased appropriately in the German language the Germans think of themselves as being *Exportweltmeister* and *Reiseweltmeister* and you detect a touch of pride when they say that, *Weltmeister* meaning world champion, with *Reise* translating into travel, in case you missed the earlier remark.

This leads me to a mean question but one that has to be asked: How well are the Germans in touch with the rest of the world? If we want to understand them we have to figure out how between the two of them one sees the other, the Germans and the rest of the world.

Isn't the country doing well? Despite the *crisis* that is much talked about in the country industry is moderately optimistic and the political establishment is not emitting any signals that a special effort may be required to stave off any looming disaster. Whilst to a thoughtful observer indications might be that a supra-human effort should be considered, none is being prepared – that is as far as is apparent if you do not have the means to go behind the scenes.

If there is anything to be alarmed about, there is no public awareness of it. Either the Germans are really cool customers or there is something there that we others, unenlightened as we may be, cannot see. Record budget deficit or not the country continues to roll along in an over-all business-as-usual mode, prompting these questions:

- What visions do the Germans have?
- What are the expectations of perfectly normal people, the politicians, captains of industry or the cultural establishment?
- Do people see the need for a turn-around of any kind?
- Don't they perhaps prefer to leave things as they are?

Interesting as it may be to look at these questions in detail there is one sobering realisation that appears to answer all of them. Somehow people believe that the government will put things right in the end. It has always done that, at least most of the time.

My attempts at taking a closer look at Germany set in before the 2005 general elections, called by the then Chancellor Gerhard Schröder. He had introduced a number of new measures, which, he may have thought, needed endorsement by the voter, given that his backing in the Bundestag had been on the decline. Fickle as ever the voter thought otherwise and elected a Christian democrat-socialist coalition government, replacing the socialists by the liberals in the next general election in 2009. That should have cleared the decks, expecting that all problems would have been solved with the country set once again for one of its impressive success stories. Yet as the dust settled we became witnesses once again to political quarrelling, the dishing out of blame and alarming shouts from some that doom is just around the corner. The disturbing realisation sprang into existence that the motor that has been driving the world's third or fourth largest economy is not running smoothly any more.

Why?

There could be a number of reasons: the operator, the fine-tuning, the fuel or perhaps all these together conspiring against Europe's flagship economy. Not being an alarmist I am nevertheless concerned, whilst many in Germany think that things are very much on the way up.

I disagree.

This work is not meant as a facts-and-figures exercise, perhaps more like insights and observations leading up to understanding - with a touch of intuition as to what could happen, if all that has already been happening continues to evolve in much the same way. On top of all else there are the really scary things that could have a significant influence on the development of the country.

We can draw parallels to Nature, when water changes its aggregate state from liquid into ice or steam. Both these phenomena occur with-a-bang, in a manner of speaking, not gradually; it is water now and ice or steam a fraction of an instant later, because some magic limit has been crossed to bring about this instantaneous change in the aggregate state. That is the part that we tend to overlook in life around us, having been accustomed to gradual change in small percentages. We perceive our daily life and all the things that come with it against and geared to a background of normality, the way they have always been. What if this normality suddenly and without warning ceases to be there?

From time to time Nature serves us with a few insights, like the events surrounding hurricane Katrina, the Haiti earthquake, the Fukushima tsunami disaster, the recent all-time record flooding caused by the rivers Elbe, Danube and their contributories in Germany or in the recent past the hurricane disaster in the Philippines. How well are we prepared if something like that were to happen again on a scale that affects an entire county, say all of Germany, not just individual regions? How would Germany cope with something of seemingly unthinkable magnitude? In addition to natural disasters let me give you just two scenarios, each of them with potentially disastrous effects on Germany:

- International demand for goods manufactured in Germany dries up; what are the economic consequences if the Exportweltmeister is confined to managing within the country's boundaries, the domestic market?

- Oil supplies become tight, for whatever reason; how well can the country cope if travel and supply logistics are confined to the sole availability of public transport, effectively by rail or ship?

Germany has come a long way since the times of turmoil, which preceded Nazi rule. The country now finds itself in the same boat with its neighbours, most if not all European countries and the world in the widest sense, facing a multitude of threats and risks on an international scale or of external origin:

- A general slowing down of world economy in the widest sense

- Growing harmful consequences of the debt crisis, Leading to growing unemployment in the world's major economies

- Increased international economic competition over markets with a shift in favour of the new emerging economies and its consequences for that of Germany

- Impending or increasing constraints affecting energy and basic resources supplies

- A looming food crisis or other events, triggering off refugee movements at an accelerated pace

- Increased occurrence of natural disasters and catastrophic weather phenomena that may be ascribed to the effects of global warming, culminating in the fear expressed by some scientists that this could lead to a new ice age

- The risk of cyber-attacks - the recent all-out cyber-attack on Latvia that for a number of days brought the country's economy and public life to a complete standstill might have been something like a dress-rehearsal to test a new weapon; do we know for certain that it was not?

- The *Risk of Eroding Public Confidence* on an international scale to the point where the general public no longer sides with the government or even turns hostile on it

- A rising tide of international terrorism emanating both from the neo-Nazi right as well as the Islamic fundamentalist left, climaxed by the rapid progress of the IS or Isis-Movement, augmented by a wide spectrum of dissatisfied to outright destructive belligerent to chaotic local citizens

The latter phenomenon is reminiscent of violent to outright bloody skirmishes of the 1930s, where Nazis fought street battles with communists. This has surfaced in other countries that have no Nazi history, including France, the Netherlands and Norway, augmented by a wide spectrum of chaotic local incidents, instigated by dissatisfied to outright destructive elements. Hamlet's words might apply to some of this, signifying 'a world out of joint'.

How will such events affect employment and the social balance within the country? Will the state continue to function smoothly or be affected by serious disruption and synergetic effects that could spiral out of control? Is there a realistic and meaningful back-up plan, if any of this happens? I worked in aviation long enough to be enlightened to the compelling logic of Murphy's Law: if something can go wrong, it will, hence prepare for it.

We perceive our daily life and all the things that come with it against and geared to a background of normality, the way they have always been. What if this normality suddenly and without warning ceases to be there? At this point I am driven to revert to German poet Heinrich Heine, having many a sleepless night thinking about Germany.

The things you may find undesirable, hard to cope with or totally unnecessary have an uncanny habit of descending on you when you can least use or afford them. Let us not overlook the fact from history that through a particular combination of circumstances Germany placed itself right at the heart of global wars, to which we have seen the need to allocate numbers.

Can a scenario of similar significance happen again?

Absurd?

Maybe not a global war but perhaps a global something else?

Unthinkable?

Napoleon's ill-fated march on Moscow defied logic and reasonable foresight as did the two World Wars and yet they happened.

For better or worse, Germany deserves our undivided attention, for Europe cannot function without it. Hence we need to understand the part that Germany plays now and will continue to play in the future, whichever way the cookie crumbles

Starting from Scratch

In Germany in May 1945 the meter was set back to zero. There remained no workable government or administrative infrastructure. That which had continued to function to the very last minute and often with deadly precision had abruptly ground to a halt. A vast part of residential, business and industrial structures had been damaged or destroyed.

Most major river crossings, railways, highways, power, gas and water supply systems had been knocked out through aerial bombardment or on-the-ground fighting. Most built-up areas had been reduced to rubble and practically nothing was working any more. Thinking of major earthquakes, floods and raging fires occurring simultaneously on a countrywide scale comes close. Hundreds of thousands of people had lost their homes through the bombing and urban house-to-house fighting. Vast numbers of refugees from the eastern parts were heading west, trying to escape capture by the advancing Soviet army. Thousands were moving about on foot through towns and villages in ruins, seeking food and shelter. It was a grim disaster scenario.

It is admirable that the Allies, pursuing the retreating German troops on German soil, swiftly took decisive steps to save the civilian population from the worst, this all the more in view of vast evidence of atrocities and war-crimes that they encountered. All the same they encouraged German volunteers and what was left of government services to re-organise and rend initial assistance under direction from the Allies.

Somehow the country pulled through and overcame the initial obstacles to start rebuilding cities, services, industries and transport systems. Considering the sheer overwhelming magnitude of the task it is remarkable how quickly many items were brought back on stream. In comparison with other disasters closer to our present time this situation was perhaps unique, helped by some special aspects: the Allies quickly set up basic food supplies and commissioned the restoring of essential services. This was a precursor to the American Marshall Plan, soon to be put into effect. Although their country was in ruins the Germans constituted a readily available, competent and effective work force, eager to bring along re-construction.

At an early date the Americans took steps towards the reconstruction of Europe. A prominent figure at the time was George Catlett Marshall, an American military leader, holding in succession the positions of Chief of Staff of the Army and Secretary of Defence. In early 1947 President Truman appointed Marshall Secretary of State. He became the spokesman for the State Department's ambitious plans to rebuild Europe. On 05 June 1947 in a speech at Harvard University he outlined 'The European Recovery Program', an American reconstruction program, which subsequently became known as 'The Marshall Plan' to help rebuild Europe and modernise its economy. For this in 1953 he was awarded the Nobel Peace Prize. West Germany became one of the major beneficiaries of this plan that had been inspired by a vision of creating a fair chance for a new Europe.

In August 1952, following in the spirit of the American Marshall Plan, the newly set up German government ruled into law the *Lastenausgleich*, burden sharing, a well-conceived financial program to raise cash and help Germany get back on its feet. The real-estate net worth of un-damaged West German properties was used as collateral for a government re-construction fund. Properties were mortgaged in favour of the government at fifty per cent of estimated worth, to be redeemed over thirty years in 120 equal quarterly instalments. It was an ingenious, bankable instrument to fuel the country's reconstruction, making start-up funding available for those who had lost everything, whilst the burden for those whose properties had been mortgaged was light at no more than 1.67 per cent p. a. of the total amount assessed.

New German businesses sprang into life in numbers and met with a limitless market, where demand often outstripped supplies and finance became increasingly available through Marshall Plan and Lastenausgleich. In terms of start-ups this was a dream scenario.

The Germans were highly motivated to make up for lost time. After having gone through the horrors of war that lay behind them they wanted to rebuild their lives, secure their own future and put their energies into something constructive.

Given the fact that the country came from a history of authoritarian rule it is all the more remarkable that the first fledglings of democratic life began to appear and spread quickly throughout the country. At this early stage it was democratisation by directive rather than driven by popular demand: the people had no own knowledge of the workings of a democracy.

Yet there was a price to pay. As the pace of reconstruction of the country quickened serious shortages in numbers became apparent of such people that were not in any way suspect of having committed war crimes or atrocities or had played a significant part in the Nazi party and its ramifications. Against initial intentions to keep the new administrative system pure and free from encumbrances from the past, standards of purity were lowered considerably. In order to restore the everyday essentials quickly parts of previous government and administrative services were re-instated, whereby in some key areas the old core structures were restored and many an old Nazi slipped back into government service.

One topic stands out in particular: government and administration in the widest sense and intertwined with it law and order. Save for minor adjustments the legal system in what was to become the new Federal Republic of Germany very much carried on as before. Even in what concerns key personnel many known Nazis came through a very superficial reform process and were implanted in the running of the new state.

In the process of rebuilding Germany only one government service emerged that was free from having had to absorb parts of former Nazi infrastructure: the new armed forces, which were set up entirely from scratch. With a view towards putting a human face on the military the phrase of the 'citizen in uniform' was coined. Looking back on the past and at the end result this has been a success. The German Bundeswehr *is* an armed force committed to serving a democratic state and is itself an institution with a democratic spirit. As a spin-off this had beneficial effects on demilitarising the police, using the example of the Bundeswehr as guidelines.

In the initial phase all police authority was vested in institutions at state level. In Nazi Germany all facets of police services had been brought together under one central command, at the top of which towered Heinrich Himmler, arguably one of the bloodiest of Hitler's cronies. In view of the role the police played in Nazi Germany many thought that there should not ever again be a federal police of any kind. However practically overnight Germany found itself right in the middle of the Cold War that had boiled up over tensions between the former eastern and western allies. In its wake the Iron Curtain became an impenetrable boundary, separating *East* from *West* and had the potential for turning into a conflict zone with the risk of shooting.

To put in certain safeguards against the accidental outbreak of hostilities between the two sides the western allies asked the West Germans to set up a special force to police the German part of the Iron Curtain, called *Zonengrenze*, literally the border between the American/British and the Soviet occupation zones. This unit like the armed forces under federal German direction was also set up from scratch and came to be known as *Bundesgrenzschutz*, the federal border police. It was also widely free from remnants of the Nazi past and was, in due course, transformed into the *Bundespolizei*, the federal police. Unavoidably, it had to come. With the disappearance of the Iron Curtain its role became increasingly that of safeguarding the country's infrastructure with a particularly visible presence at Germany's airports. It has increasingly taken on an anti-terrorism role, in which it made an impressive debut at Mogadishu, Somalia, with the successful freeing of a hijacked Lufthansa airliner.

The Bundeswehr and the Bundespolizei are two reassuring positive elements of a country that is committed to grow into a solid democracy. It would be unfair to expect total overnight success but given what lies behind Germany they are doing admirably well.

Today Germany is a staunch ally and trusted friend of the West. Its commitment to values shared in NATO and the European institutions stands head and shoulders above doubt. Isn't it therefore sacrilege to analyse and discuss the country's role and sift through detail, instead of accepting things the way they are with no ifs and buts? The answer to this question must be a whole-hearted 'no'. In a free society you not only have a right to take a closer look; it may even become your obligation to strive for an ever better understanding with those that are on your side. It will make the relationship stronger.

My attention focuses on those aspects in the conduct of nations, where Germany followed a distinctively different route from that of its neighbours. In 1945 Germany emerged from a 2,000 year history of authoritarian rule, which had shaped social awareness and citizenship or, conversely, the lack thereof. In 1914 a few pistol shots were enough to light the fuse of smouldering resentment and ill feelings, exploding into a World War that plunged the world into chaos and misery. Hardly any of this can be blamed on the individual citizens. However, they had allowed their country to slip into an undercurrent of hate. In 1933 that undercurrent was resuscitated and in 1939 brought to a cataclysmic climax.

The German national environment has evolved through the time-frame of two millennia, in which the emphasis was biased in favour of the state, the dogma of states' rights breaking those of the individual. What society or country can come through 2,000 years of this and remain totally unaffected? People shape countries, countries shape people and an authoritarian environment has left its mark. To do the Germans justice we may have to exercise patience for some time to come.

When the Federal Republic of Germany was created its instigators ran up against a number of very basic, practical issues. There were far too few people on hand that had not somehow been part of the former governmental system and been influenced by it. People were given a new set of blueprints, but that which had been ingrained in their heart and soul was still there, subconsciously creeping into many a facet of the new Germany.

No one should doubt the sincerity of today's Germans and their government and its institutions. Yet, there always is a spirit that runs through fabric and fibre of a country that can be felt in numerous instances. In the case of Germany – this is entirely my subjective, personal judgment – the spirit that reverberates in the country does not reflect a cheerful, positive atmosphere, like in saying we'll get on top of whatever it is. This comes out in daily life even without trying very hard. When you present a new idea to a German, his likely first reaction may be *das geht nicht - that won't work* whilst the American might react with a cheerful *how can I help you?* Afterwards, the American may not really help you and the German will somehow make things work. It is the attitude that comes through in spontaneous, first reactions that somehow determines the climate.

The Mahagonny Syndrome

In the face of overwhelming evidence that it is already too late and all is lost, looking at today's Germany we are reminded of the ancient, time honoured art, practiced again and again, of people as well as whole governments, carrying on regardless and seemingly enjoying themselves, doing so. As bad as that? Well, maybe, tongue in cheek, to stir up interest.

Some years after World War I German composer Kurt Weil and writer Bert Brecht may have felt compelled that action was needed to draw attention to the situation the country was in and wrote the opera *The Rise and Fall of the City of Mahagonny*. To appease the critics and play it down, so as to facilitate general acceptance, they called it a *Singspiel*, a theatrical play with music. It was first performed in Leipzig, Germany, on 09 March 1930 and subsequently banned under Hitler. At the time its authors wanted to portray the state of affairs that had taken hold of Germany after the end of World War I, coupled with a passionate plea to listen to the voices of reason and insight. The general idea is as much a perfect fit for post World War II Germany as it had been for that of post World War I, for which it had been originally intended. It runs along these lines and I want to boldly offer it as

The Mahagonny Syndrome

Typical founder situations often extend over three generations. The mothers and fathers work their fingers to the bone. The daughters and sons slacken the pace and excel at discovering the merits of leisure and the satisfaction derived from excelling at being undeclared champions at world travel. The generation of the grand-children doesn't have the remotest idea any more where all the wealth came from and that at some time somebody had to work hard to accumulate it. Their horizons do not extend beyond that which they can touch with their outstretched arms. They are boxed in by epitomising self, here and now. Their quest is to 'find themselves', whatever may lie behind that figure of speech. They escape into adventure, take to 'danger-seeking' and lose themselves in occult excess. Their society in its evolution runs from departure to new horizons, through complacent saturation and ends in its catastrophic downfall.

Brecht and Weil came up with the fictitious City of Mahagonny, imagined to be in some unnamed banana-republic but actually meaning somewhere in Germany, going through a comparable phase in its development. Its downfall and impending catastrophe were there for all to see. Despite concerned voices of caution nobody cared, nobody took notice, let alone made preparations to stave off disaster so that its eventual annihilation became unavoidable.

If we try to use this example today, attempting to arouse people's interest, they are not even remotely interested.

"Not here."

"Why the hell not?"

"Because it's all different, not like what you are talking about."

You get a similar reaction if you mention the great economic crisis of 1929 or the demise of the Weimar Republic, that brief interval of democratic governance in Germany that was sandwiched between the rule of Kaiser and Hitler, respectively. If you give people an example from history, relating it to the actual situation and the inherent alarming parallels, they will be quick to dismiss it, turning around your good-intentioned argument until they find some insignificant point of detail, on which they can prove you wrong, using that as justification why they should not listen to you in the first place. Rather than politely thanking you, potentially saving their lives, people will put more energies into arguing why they should *not* take any action, even going beyond that and doing whatever they can to silence you.

My allusions to the Mahagonny Syndrome are by no means a subjective appraisal of the condition in which the country finds itself. I am driven by the realisation that large segments of the population are vigorously charging ahead with a vengeance on a course to self-destruct in pursuit of wealth, while another even larger segment through the harsh conditions that have been brought about is driven into a self-compounding process of establishing wide-spread poverty. We can deliver proof to the rigorous standards of modern science that many facets of our life have become or are in the process of becoming unsustainable. Only a bold and determined change in our attitudes and ambitions can help to secure a meaningful future for our children and future generations.

Let us recap the situation.

First here is the good news. This is how the Germans like to see themselves in some fields that are currently of particular interest, where Germany performs better than average or even the rest of the world:

- Over the last few decades Germany has been ranking among the world's top ten economies, sometimes the top five or even the top three to four

- Germany has been maintaining a sustained active trade balance

- By international comparison Germany has been enjoying one of the lowest levels of unemployment

- On top of that youth unemployment is one of the lowest in Europe

- Trade relations between industry and workforce on the whole have been good with only minor incidences of industrial action

- Germany is playing a steady role in secure energy production, gradually replacing nuclear power generating plant by innovative alternative technologies

This rather brilliant picture deserves closer scrutiny because on the other hand there is the not so good news:

- In the early 1970s Germany's GDP 'went negative' and has remained there ever-since; put into pseudo-scientific language that means that the aggregate total of national income does not meet the aggregate total of national expenditure; Germany has adopted debt finance in order to balance the books or in other words the national budget, *borrowing money* rather than making up the gap from *earned income*.

- As a consequence, Germany has settled into accepting a running annual budget deficit and a national debt with an accrued aggregate total *well* above €2,000,000,000,000 as at mid-2012 and rising - I mentioned that.

- No politically accepted and duly ratified plan is on record as to how this is *ever* going to be repaid, who is going to do the re-paying and who is left out in the cold if there is no re-payment forthcoming.

- Despite that the country has been maintaining an active foreign trade balance, made possible by the fact that there exists a hidden gap that is closed by somebody else's money, i. e. debt.

On the outside that may look like good news. On closer scrutiny it means that Germany has been selling its exports below cost, which invites the challenge of price dumping on a national and international grand scale. Germany should have generated more tax or other national income, which it continues to dodge with determination

Let me phrase this differently: since the 1970s Germany has been continuously maintaining inadequate levels of taxation for the benefit of its international competitiveness, meeting budget deficits by increasing debt. Much of this debt is held by its own banks or banks under its jurisdiction, putting an additional slant on the process.

Germany has been consolidating its international competitiveness by replacing high-cost domestic suppliers of goods and services by cheaper providers, engaging in international production sharing on a considerable scale, irrespective of repercussions for domestic socio-economic consequences. That means that industrial development and orientation has been placing private capital interests over those of general well-being of the national economy, in other words: the country and its citizens. *Raubtier* or predator-capitalism has been outperforming the earlier maxims of social market-economy, which formed the backbone of Germany's post-World War II economic rise.

After the end of the so-called 'boom-years' Germany *did* build up a high level of unemployment. This was partly offset by an overall reduction in the disposable work force, made possible by the effects of retirement vs. reduced influx of domestic workers due to a declining birth-rate. Despite that there is considerable unemployment, masked in part by vast numbers of people being in state funded so-called 'programs', working short time or in subsidised low-income subsistence employment. By contrast: the benefits from this state of affairs accrue to the affluent few, the ones that own and have and reap the benefits from other people's toil. We are looking at a classic capitalistic situation, such as has previously led to clashes if not revolutions.

Internationally one hears little criticism of Germany, hardly any, as if people were frightened of any negative consequences for themselves, if they were to openly voice concern or even protest. The German position is a very short-sighted one. I call that *King*

Midas Syndrome, signifying self-destruction through greed and self-ishness. It constitutes a wrong on two fronts:

- Domestically, within the country, the rich get richer and the poor poorer. It is not a uniquely German phenomenon, but the Germans are particularly good at it - as usual, I am tempted to say, for whatever the Germans do, they do it to perfection.

- Internationally the Germans' policy of ramming through interests of their own, regardless of what this does to others, has only got a limited shelf-life. Sooner or later they will be taken to task by the rest of the world. No good merchant will bleed his customers dry and live on to enjoy it for very long.

There are two disturbing examples of how the Germans balanced the books, albeit by default rather than their own achievement and with the clemency of others:

- At the end of World War I Germany was bankrupt and the rest of the world was left to suffer grave consequences. Some reparations in respect of war damages were levied by the victors; a very small portion, but nowhere near enough nor on an adequate scale was paid by the Germans.

- At the end of World War II Germany was even more bankrupt, having charged ahead on burning up the assets stolen from countries they had occupied and from destroying their economies. This time the Americans went a long way towards closing the gap, for which the Germans never really thanked them.

In neither of these cases have the Germans been overly concerned over what they did. They have largely been forgiven by the world and allowed to have another go. Whilst some German individuals and industries have been able to amass great fortunes the country, technically speaking, is bankrupt even today. What happens if someone shouts: I want to have my money back!? We need to include this aspect when trying to assess the danger potential.

A Crushing Legacy – The Authoritarian State

Let me race you through an outline of German history over the time from the Roman Empire to today, a little over 2,000 years, promising to get back to some interesting points of detail in due course. As we go back over the centuries, German history is marked by the prevalence of authoritarian rule and a complete absence of Democracy of any shape or colour.

That sets apart Germany from its neighbours with their democratic history and traditions. *L'état c'est moi*, I am the state, was the mantra of rulers in countries with an authoritarian form of government, which in the Germanic parts of Europe and in particular after the proclamation of the German Empire formed the basis of state philosophy under the banner of *Staatsraison*, state supremacy, whereby those in power had all rights and ordinary citizens none.

Authoritarian rulers imposed laws that were not reconcilable with an innate sense of justice. To uphold them they needed to lay down formal, written law that simply by invoking sovereign powers would outrank fundamental basic rights and could be held up in court regardless of circumstances, if need be.

To tighten their grip on the country the rulers would engage in illicit actions that seemingly benefit the state but run counter to a sense of justice. If you adhere to authoritarian principles for long, it is only a small step to dictatorship or fascism. What follows is the lack of citizenship, embedded in a culture of selfishness and insufficient tolerance of diverging views. Over time there is little preparedness to agree unless compelled to do so through the fear of punishment. In a climate of authoritarian rule the ability to prioritise and a motivating positive spirit are lost. Instead of clear-cut distinctions between right and wrong undercurrents run through processes that on the outside appear *normal* but are inherently unjust.

The authoritarian state relied on punishment and reward. Free countries rely on reason and insight that motivate the citizen to respect the state and abide by the law.

Let us be candid:

Germany has not been a champion of Democracy.

Not ever.

As someone with a predominantly scientific background I would say that a period of fifteen over a history of some 2,000 years makes that a negligible quantity at a mere 0.75%, or three quarters of a percentage point. The period 1918 to 1933 of the so called *Weimar Republic,* following on the heels of World War I, was the only time Germany had democratic government, albeit one that was neither respected nor cared for by the Germans at the time. It came to be known by the name 'Weimar' as the seat of government was moved to the city of that name.

What stood out most, were the different avenues that the development of Germany and that of its neighbours had followed. A work by Dr. Ruediger Tessmann[1], an accomplished scientist and keen historian, very thoroughly deals with this aspect of the history of Germany. The devastating truth can be found in the first chapter of his work on the subject.

In the year 09 AD a man called Herman, Principal Chief of the Germanic tribe of the Cheruscans, defeated a large Roman expeditionary force, a highly trained and well-equipped army of some 15,000 men. That meant three complete legions out of the Roman Empire's total military strength at the time of – estimated - twenty-eight legions. Under their commander Quinctilius Varus they had set out to explore the until then not very well known lands of northern *Germania Magna,* to assess their potential for being added to the already vast possessions of the Roman Empire. The event went down in history as The Battle of the Teutoburg Forest, much glorified in the period of the German Empire of the *Kaiser,* the emperor, and elevated during Nazi rule in Germany to being the one deciding event in the history of the country.

The more or less official German version runs as follows: Herman was a national hero, who saved the country from the threat of foreign rule, once and for all, the Germans' ultimate hero, no ifs and buts.

---

[1]Tessmann, Dr Ruediger – "German History Seen Through the Country's Literature" - "Die Geschichte der Deutschen im Spiegel ihrer Literatur", Albenga 2008

Tessmann saw the matter from a slightly different angle. Herman or *Herrmann der Cherusker*, the German way, known by the Romans as Arminius Cheruscus, was actually an officer in the Roman army, who along with his Cheruscan tribesmen had been conscripted into the Roman army, then defected and ambushed his former employer, to steal the war-chest of the Roman expeditionary force to Germania. Being a brilliant soldier, bordering on reckless, knowing the terrain and playing his advantages to the fullest, Arminius dealt the Romans a crushing defeat of such proportions that for centuries to come they made no further attempt at colonising that part of the world. In practical terms that means that all of what the Romans called Germania Magna was left untouched by them, to follow its own chosen course.

Thus for about 800 years most of the territories east of the river Rhine and north of the river Danube developed in their own, Germanic way. Whilst most of the rest of Europe, in particular Italy, France, the Netherlands, Spain and Britain, shared much of the cultural heritage of the sophisticated Roman Empire, the rest of Germania, not occupied by the Romans, stayed firmly rooted in the somewhat sombre Germanic tribal and language culture, where their gods Wotan or Odin, Thor, Loki and a whole host of others were still widely revered.

If it had not been for Arminius, Roman occupation of and rule over all that was eventually to become Germany would have covered the whole country and the blessings of Roman civilisation would have reached the shores of the Baltic Sea then and there. Who knows to what end? But that is of course entirely academic. Most of future Germany remained deeply entrenched in the Germanic culture, over which towered their gods, appearing as a rather violent and savage bunch. Whilst their Roman and Greek counterparts Jupiter, Zeus, Apollo and all the others pursued happiness on the home front and are known primarily for their conquests of outstanding, beautiful and otherwise remarkable women, their Germanic cousins of sorts saw no nobler task than to fight; to the death, if necessary. There was never a happy-end in their stories and sagas and the ultimate climax was to be the *Ragnaroeck*, the end of the world, when *Fenrir*, the giant hound from hell, would break his chains and start the final combat, after which all would be over and time would end then and there – without any future above and beyond that.

I am referring to this at length, because the Germans in their heritage had 800 years more of this than the rest of Europe. Might not that explain a thing or two? Nobody is talking about justifying, just explaining.

Over the centuries, following the adoption of the Christian faith by the Roman Empire, round about the year 300 AD, Christianisation gradually spread throughout most of Europe. In its wake the Germanic territories west of the Rhine and south of the Danube adopted the Christian faith about the year 390 AD.

By contrast, most of the rest of Germania Magna was not converted to Christianity until centuries later. In 785 AD Emperor Charles the Great, Charlemagne, defeated the Saxons under their *King Wiedekind* and had 4,500 of their noblemen publicly beheaded, just to underscore the point that he was really serious about things, which earned him the dubious honour of being called *The Butcher of the Saxons*. To me this serves as a milestone event of what the Germanic cultural heritage brought to the table in what was to become the heartlands of Europe:

In a nutshell – it was bloody.

Christianisation in those days was no laughing matter and your choice was to adopt the faith or die. Parts of northern Germania held out until about 840 AD. In 722 AD a father Bonifacius had tried to convert the Frisians, a Germanic tribe. To demonstrate the superiority of Christianity he chopped down a holy oak, dedicated to god Thor, but the Frisians were unimpressed and simply killed him, which prompted the Church in Rome to elevate him to Saint.

Being concerned primarily with tightening its grip on all of Europe, the Church turned out to be an enthusiastic ally in bringing everybody to heel on the understanding that it was the highest – ultimately God-given – authority in the land, which was emphasised with a heavy hand, not shying away from rather generous bloodshed if deemed conducive to their ultimate goal. Thus, in Central Europe by the end of the ninth century AD you were either a Christian or dead.

In 841 AD the *Holy Roman Empire of the German Nation of Charles the Great*, informally created as things evolved from tribal culture to empire, was divided amicably between his nephews Ludwig and Karl into a western and an eastern part, which in due course and following totally different routes were to become France and Germany, respectively. These were as yet by no means nation states but rather territories under an umbrella, held by the man at the top, who had to do his utmost to project power throughout his land. There were still tribal and language divisions and rivalries between the various local and regional chiefs and rulers.

After the division of the Empire the two parts followed distinctly different routes. That which was to become France, the western part, drew on the roots of Roman rule and culture with the effect that French, the language that emerged, bears clearly recognisable resemblances to its Latin origins, whilst the eastern parts were completely devoid of such influences.

Europe settled into a power structure which to ordinary mortals showed God at the top with the pope and the emperor just a tiny bit underneath – not all that much – and presiding over the lords spiritual and temporal. Below that your only option was to obey. To the obedient vast majority this meant the comfort of a clearly ordered society, whilst enlightened spirits like Galileo practised their science under the constant threat of death by torture. Those were by no means happy times in medieval Europe and absolutely not conducive to the progress of the sciences and general knowledge, resulting there from.

Things did not really get a whole lot better as a result of Martin Luther's reformation, which split the Church in two and created the Protestant variant of the faith. It is true that he re-directed the focus of religious attention back at the basics. But his teachings did not do a lot for the common man, who switched one form of oppression for another, if his ruler opted to convert to the Protestant faith. At this time power lay to a great extent in the hands of the aristocracy and the emperor was dependent on their co-operation. For the nobles there was an incentive to turn their backs on Catholicism as that meant escaping from taxation by the Church, which was powerless to stop this. Luther's teachings were a godsend to the nobility, allowing them to shake off taxation by the Church in Rome.

Luther preached that all and any authority is God-given and to be strictly obeyed, but at common-man-level it didn't make a blind bit of difference whether you obeyed the pope, the emperor or your local nobleman, as long as you did the obeying. Luther has a lot to answer for in conjunction with authoritarian rule. He was also openly anti-Semitic and showered the peasant farmers with contempt, who were reeling under pressure from above. Adding my totally personal and entirely unscientific observation I would sum up: Luther's teachings were all but a barrel of fun for the ordinary little chap.

Out of the tense situation that arose in the wake of the Reformation erupted The Thirty-Year War in the Germanic territories, which lasted from 1618 to 1648 and reduced the population of the country from about eighteen to six million, devastated the cities and all but wiped out agriculture.

The year 1667, nineteen years after *The Thirty-Year War*, marks a milestone event in German history with the emergence of Prussia. Defeating the Swedes, who had stayed in the Germanic territories after the end of the war, the *Grosse Kurfuerst*, ruler of the principality, later to become the *Kingdom of Brandenburg*, threw them off the land and extended his territory up to the Baltic Sea, with its new capital at Potsdam, at a time, when Berlin was no more than a village in a swampy, insect-infested area some twenty miles up the river.

From Brandenburg emerged Prussia, which was to become the motor of a rising German national spirit. It is closely linked with its rulers, *King Friedrich Wilhelm I*, called *The Soldier King*, for having drilled his army to become an awe-inspiring fighting machine, and *King Friedrich II*, called *The Great*, who carried on much in the same spirit. They brought together all that was devoid of joy and pleasure in the Germanic heritage and in Protestantism, to epitomise austerity, duty and hard work, dedication to king and country and obedience – to the death, if necessary. Although they modelled their cultural life on that of France and spoke more French than German their footprint was Teutonic. After son Friedrich of King Friedrich II had tried to escape from his father's tough and heavy-handed rule together with his closest friend Katte and been apprehended at the border, he was forced by his father to witness the beheading of his friend in the prison courtyard.

That very much reflects the stuff that Prussia was made of: God-fearing, protestant, absolutely unforgiving, unsmiling and ice-cold. There was not even a whisper of Democracy to be heard anywhere near or signs of it seen. In fairness it has to be said that they did, in due course, turn out to be champions and patrons of the arts and the advancement of science, doing so seriously, unsmiling and striving for and enhancing to whatever extent possible efficiency and perfection at what you were doing, regardless of whether or not you enjoyed it.

Whilst the eighteenth century saw such spectacular events as The French Revolution and American Independence nothing on a similar scale happened in the German territories, in which there existed as yet no Germany as a nation state but a multitude of principalities, free cities and no fewer than four kingdoms: Saxony, Prussia, Wuerttemberg and the Principality that was to become the Kingdom of Bavaria.

Habsburg or Austria was already in the emerging Austro-Hungarian camp, with plans and an Emperor of its own, who traced his authority back to the Holy Roman Empire of the German Nation. Out of the French Revolution arose the rule of Napoleon, bringing under its reign and occupying vast parts of Europe. This may have provided one of the first significant incentives towards the formation of Germany as a nation state, as there emerged wide-spread preparedness to unite, to shake off foreign domination. The fight against Napoleon's troops brought diverse forces in Germany together that wanted to chase the French off German soil.

In 1806 Napoleon's army defeated the Prussians in *The Battle of Jena and Auerstedt*. In 1813 the Prussians got back at them and came out victorious in *The Battle of Leipzig*, which marked the end of Napoleonic rule and the from that point onwards unstoppable rise of Prussia, to become the leading power factor in the hemisphere of future Germany. Somewhere along the way we have the ultimate defeat of French attempts at resurgence in *The Battle of Waterloo*, which saw the English and the Prussians and a host of others united to finish off the French, once and for all.

In 1871 the Proclamation of the *Second German Empire* with Kaiser Wilhelm I, also being the King of Prussia, as its first absolute ruler united again after a long time most German lands under one rule, marking the beginning of the period that was to usher in dramatic change. The end of the *Thirty-Year War* in 1648 *de facto* had also meant the inglorious end of the Holy Roman Empire of the German Nation, the First Reich, which over most if not all of its existence had never been an effective, centralised power structure. It continues to appear in some history books up to the proclamation of the Second Empire with effectively nothing to its credit;

take this as my totally unscientific and somewhat cynical personal view.

In the run-up to and following the defeat of the French in 1813 there had been a nationalistic undercurrent in Germany. In 1848 a national assembly was convened at Saint Paul's Cathedral in Frankfurt. This culminated in an attempt at proclaiming Democracy in Germany. It was led predominantly by prominent citizens and eminent thinkers. They failed to get popular support. The aristocracy refused to support them, adamant on maintaining their privileged role, and the movement collapsed. Throughout German history from the year 0 AD and up to the end of World War I that was and remained to be the only serious, albeit totally unsuccessful effort at establishing a democratic state on German soil.

Just to emphasise the point: little Iceland out in the North Atlantic draws on the same cultural roots as do the Germans, in one way or another, but they have had Democracy for a few hundred years and never anything else in recent times, the lucky bastards.

Following wide-spread popular unrest in the wake of the harsh conditions brought about with the end of World War I the Kaiser abdicated, clearing the path for The Weimar Republic, an ultimately failed attempt at establishing democratic rule in Germany. With the country still reeling from the shock inflicted by World War I and its aftermath the terrain was ripe for Hitler to usurp power and there was nobody there to stop him from doing it. The existence of the Weimar Republic ceased with hardly more than a decade-and-a-half of widely unsupported and thereby futile efforts. The Germans as a people failed to embrace the concept of Democracy, their only opportunity ever over a period of some 2,000 years. Not supported by the nobility or the masses with only a dedicated few rallying behind it failure was unavoidable.

The rest is well-known history. Germany was defeated in World War II. In a constitutional assembly on 23 May 1949 the German states that had emerged after the end of the war on the soil of West Germany adopted and signed the *Grundgesetz - Basic Law*, which was to be the constitution of the country and marked the formation of the Federal Republic of Germany. This happened very much under the auspices of the Western Allies that had defeated Germany in World War II. People in Germany were still struggling to make ends meet. Political life, which in the initial stages had been carried very much by such outstanding personalities as

Konrad Adenauer, the First Chancellor of the Federal Republic, developed only slowly, whilst the day-to-day functioning of the state and public life still very much depended on and employed structures and institutions that had survived from the previous regime; this means of course Nazi Germany.

On 21 June 1948 the German currency was devalued and replaced by the Deutsche Mark, short D-Mark or DM, which was soon to become a symbol of German strength and a yard-stick for the country's recovery. In 1968 the mood in the country erupted in open protest, predominantly from the student movement that wanted to see significant changes in numerous points of law and practical matters that affected daily life. Public mood had caught up with the fact that there were still too many remnants in everyday life and in government from the Nazi period. Over the next decade and beyond there were many changes; the American Marshall Plan had provided cash injections to re-start industry and the country went from strength to strength.

Whilst there was unprecedented growth, signs were becoming apparent that not all was as good as it could be, marking a gradual transition of the country. Creating the European Union to replace the European Economic Community, German Unification and the effects of globalisation were to change the picture.

If anything was lacking in Germany it was grass-roots Democracy. There is precious little in Germany's past on which to base the hope for its prevalence. For centuries the prudent survival strategy had been:

- Practice a trade, the arts or commerce, be good at it and pay your taxes

- Don't come to the attention of those above you unless the news is good – in their eyes

- And do what those above you demand of you, enthusiastically and without complaining

Authoritarian rule was the only form of government that people knew from history as it manifested itself to the common man. And even the upper crust was never entirely safe from deliberate acts in which those at the very top indulged. If it pleased them the country went to war and you had to support the war effort. There was not an awful lot of room for civil courage, let alone civil disobedience, which would have been high treason and most likely punishable by death.

Thus the liberation of Germany from Nazi rule by the Allies was in effect the country's first meaningful contact with Democracy, save for the brief episode of the Weimar Republic. During the Nazi period there were brave attempts to overthrow Hitler by maybe a handful of high ranking officers in the German armed forces, mostly members of the aristocracy. But they were too few in number and lacked wide-spread support. Actually, they lacked support of any kind. Things might have turned out differently if there had been a collective memory of good things, worth aspiring to and a spirit of Democracy up in the air, somewhere, maybe as a dream from history. But the country was never fortunate enough to enjoy that and had to suffer the consequences — to the bitter end, for the second time in less than half a century.

So over the last two thousand years the Federal Republic is the best political system that the Germans have ever experienced. It may not be the perfect model of a state nor of a solid democracy. But it can be improved, streamlined or adjusted, whatever it takes. It will be worth doing, for there is nothing better on the horizon. Maybe, in view of all the bad news from the past, the Germans deserve full praise for having persevered.

Shadows of the Past

Sooner or later it dawns on most of us that nothing in life is ever all good or all bad. Even when you are striving for the good there often are opposing forces pulling in different directions until one or the other prevails and the over-all result meets with the necessary acceptance and support. The scientist might say that the aggregate total is constant, give or take a little. I cannot offer any educated proof for such a statement, yet I do not think that it should be necessary. Often that which comes across as unacceptable or bad balances out something that otherwise might be too good to be true. We have come to know and accept this situation as competition, which at times may lead to better results. In that respect the *good* in life may be competing with the *bad*, each of the two trying to be the dominating force. Sometimes one of them wins, sometimes it's the other. But there may be limits to such an unbiased openness.

One of the darkest sides of German history immediately catches up with us. There is their penchant for perfectionism in large-scale operations like starting wars and, towering above all else, the horrific concept of concentration camps. At the core of these is the notion that 'an-order-from-above' relinquishes own personal responsibility, thereby shielding someone following orders from acquiring personal guilt. This may explain but never justify some of the horrendous evil deeds committed. Heartless cruelty is not something specifically German. We find it in all cultures, all walks of life and at all times in history. That which strikes me as specifically German is the ice-cold perfectionism, with which they add that extra bit of dedication. If an order was given to carry out an evil deed - no matter how evil - those receiving it would carry it out. Perhaps we can see it as having been embedded in German heritage, something that over centuries had come to be considered the right thing to do.

The human species can be a savage beast, as has been demonstrated in many parts of the world and in numerous countries. What is frightening about what happened under German rule in the 1930s to mid-1940s are the scale, the merciless and seemingly blind execution and the complete absence of any rationality in conjunction with these events. It is as if there exist characteristics in people in Germany that can function seemingly automatically, if the orders are given.

That is frightening.

This does not necessarily relate to anything that is specifically German. It may be the unfortunate coming together of highly advanced skills and abilities, insufficiently developed rationality and a human environment that has not been reached by a deep sense of caring, charity and mercy. The Germans had the misfortune to combine all of this to negative perfection.

One of the buzz-words of the Germans is *Ordnung,* best translated as meaning that there exists a recognisable and generally accepted order of things. If you translate it as *order* that does not quite match what is meant when you use the word in the English language. That is why I prefer not to translate it. *Ordnung* is not objective and in a negative sense has a moral or ethical connotation, albeit hidden. The hidden aspect can best be explained as it is not about being right or wrong, it is about 'structuring with a specific intent'. In other words: it is deliberate and intentional and does not flow out of a person's natural inclinations for doing things.

Order as defined in the English language exists when the apples are in one basket and the pears in another. By contrast order graduates to becoming Ordnung when there exists a theory, dogma or policy statement attached to it, meaning that everything is in its *defined* or *intended* appropriate place or where it should be by deliberate definition and not a natural order of things. The opposite of Ordnung is Unordnung, the absence of Ordnung, one such case being apples and pears in the same basket or, worse, scattered all over the floor.

For the Germans there exists an extra twist to it:

I would rather have left this point aside but its understanding is a prerequisite to figuring out the Germans. They love Ordnung and detest Unordnung. In recent history, going back to the Third Reich and the Nazis, *Ordnung machen,* to create Ordnung, could have included ridding the country of those of its citizens that had been declared to be undesirables. In this group the rulers of the day included Jews, which under the so called Nuremburg Racial Laws, concerning the preservation of the purity of the Arian race, were deprived of their rights of citizenship, culminating in their right to exist; but also socialists, communists and other groups. Suitable legislation was processed through the Reichstag, at that time a mere rubber-stamping pseudo-parliamentarian body for the Nazis, as legal basis for their persecution of certain groups of people. This meant that actions against these groups served the maintenance of Ordnung.

Thus, the total cynicism was that the Nazi regime was predicated on the implementation of Ordnung, thereby maintaining a semblance of legality. In our eyes today these race laws were phoney laws but they were nevertheless enforced. For the average German who had been raised with respect for the law that created a dilemma.

The thing that stands out here is that even those horrible Nazis sought to maintain a seemingly correct form, the appearances of legality, regardless of the fact that the form was constituted by and based on phoney laws. They existed in print, were stamped, signed and sealed and stated that certain basic fundamental human rights had been abolished; among them were the right of certain groups of people to live in peace and engage in the pursuit of happiness, let alone the mere right to go on living, if it was your misfortune to be among those singled out by the Nazis under these laws. Their rights were subjugated to a stack of paper, concocted at the behest of a criminally evil government but implemented thoroughly and to the point by the human resources of the state. We know of other countries, where human rights were violated, but I cannot think of one where this was done with such heartless and brutal dedication.

This point is a hard one to stomach. If something is in the book, the law book, that holds magic power over the Germans. We all know about the at times supra-human efforts by today's Germany as a country and the Germans as individuals to come to terms with the past. There is hardly anybody alive in Germany today and definitely nobody in any government office that had a hand in those dreadful things of the past. The Germans deserve full credit for their sincerity in dealing with the country's past.

The reason why I bring this up is because it points towards one of the country's great weaknesses: the – at times slavish – adherence to something that is put before the Germans that bears the hallmarks of governmental authority, something in writing that cites laws or legally binding regulations. This is by no means something new. Germany's great poet Johann Wolfgang von Goethe, dealing with the relationship between the ordinary person and authority, wrote in his drama Faust: *denn was er schwarz auf weiss besitzt, kann er getrost nach Hause tragen,* which translates freely into that which is given in black-and-white, in writing, is beyond doubt.

This still looms large over the country, even today: They want everything in writing. The underlying reason for this is fear. It is something very basic. Be prepared that the Germans will throw the book at you and no matter how good your intentions, you will have to justify your actions; it helps if you can cite a point of law. And make sure you bring the book along and know on which page to open it.

This last topic is intertwined with one of the qualities of the Germans. When push comes to shove they stand their ground, provided that ground is clearly defined and they know the legal basis on which they stand. If that is clear, they don't run, they don't panic and everybody will do his or her job for as long as this is humanly possible. They are dependable to the end. They show up on time, work the hours or more and will do their utmost with what is expected of them. And if need be they will go the extra mile.

This is a distinct virtue - up to a point, the point being that at some stage there has to be the provision for a rational assessment, when to hold out and when to cut and run. In World War II in the siege of Stalingrad in the Soviet Union the German army held out to the bitter end, until all that was left was to surrender unconditionally. At the beginning of World War II the British sent the so called Expeditionary Force to France, assisting the French to fight the Germans. When the situation became untenable the British troops were given the order to try and make it back to England by whatever means possible.

So, the Brits did a runner? I don't think so. Using anything that could float and under fire from the Germans they evacuated some 330,000 British, French and Belgian troops across the English Channel. These were to be an invaluable asset in the further course of the war. At Stalingrad the Germans under direct orders from Hitler to hold out to the last bullet lost about 150,000 men, wounded or killed in action. Only about 100,000 survived the fighting and went into captivity, of which fewer than about a tenth returned to Germany, long after the end of the war and too late to contribute to the re-birth of the country at an early and decisive stage.

A British friend of mine who had been right in the middle of the evacuation of the British troops at Dunkirk in France summed it up with these words. We like to say: 'the fighting man who runs away will live to fight another day'. It is important to have a clear understanding of when it is more important to preserve human life, save lives, rather than to hold out on points of principle and perish to no good end and nothing tangible to show for it.

Let's face it: the British and their allies won the war. The conclusion that I want to draw from that is that the Germans will be your faithful ally but at times you have to give them guidance – when they have problems sorting out their priorities.

This might be the moment to question the Germans' lack of rationality, their unpreparedness to place rational thought over dogmatic adherence to principle. Let me try to bring out the point:

- If you engage in criminal activities but are intelligent and brilliant about it you are a smart criminal.

- If you engage in criminal activities in strict adherence to a set of principles, allowing this to outperform your stated criminal objective, you are a stupid criminal.

The Nazis were unbelievably stupid criminals, dedicating huge resources to activities that were running counter to their war effort, like persecuting parts of the population, heavy-handedly alienating people that would otherwise have been inclined to side with and help them.

There will always be those who manage to put a wrong twist to things you say. I want to emphasise that the Nazis deserved nothing more than to be defeated in their criminal onslaught. But if they had thought the thing through rationally they should have come to the conclusion that many of their activities were totally counterproductive, like dedicating vast manpower and other resources to hunting down members of the Jewish community, which in terms of potentially winning the war ran seriously counter to any such plans. Despite the hard and bitter truth today we can say thank God for that. Ultimately it was their own stupidity that helped by a long way to bring down the Nazis.

My grave concern is that this is not something specifically Nazi. It is specifically authoritarian and absolutely undemocratic. It has survived in some quarters, in principle or in spirit, in elements of the German state and in public life. That is cause for concern. It means that in Germany bold upright courage and civil disobedience are not likely to come to the fore. When it comes to the crunch do not expect acts of individual bravery running up against the heavy hand of authority. Champions of good and courageous causes stand to be left out in the cold or hung out to dry.

Do not expect to find a preponderance of enlightened, critical approach to daily life. Remember: they have the book and you had better know what's in it. Once something has been written and is available in print that counts. I am repeating myself but this is practically the law supreme and one of the key issues of what runs the country.

Don't forget!

Of course, this may be a good moment to bring up the fact that there can also be good news. You will not do the Germans justice if you fail to acknowledge their preparedness to engage in acts of outstanding solidarity. There is something very remarkable that has been happening on the quiet, in an unspectacular and seemingly natural way. Let me give you the bare facts:

- On 8 November 1948, the *Notopfer Berlin* (emergency relief for Berlin) was passed into law to raise funds for helping Berlin as the isolated outpost, surrounded by Communist dominated East Germany. A highly visible measure was to require a DM 0.02 solidarity stamp to be attached on any letter sent through the German postal system; this seems small but it raised millions.

- On 14 August 1952 the Bundestag, the federal German parliament, then still that of West Germany, passed into law the Lastenausgleich - burden sharing, mentioned earlier

- After German re-unification in October 1990 the Bundestag, now representing all of Germany, including the new states that used to make up East Germany, passed legislation whereby a solidarity tax was added to income tax payable, labelled Solidaritaetszuschlag, income tax solidarity supplement, to raise additional funding for the cost of German Unification.

None of these measures met with any significant disapproval, let alone protest, the basis for their imposition was generally accepted as justified and people paid without complaining. You can add to this a general preparedness in the country to accept and integrate refugees from other countries, in particular after the Hungarian Uprising in 1968 and as a consequence of The Balkan Wars. My guess is that there is something in the German soul that says 'we've been there ourselves, let's help the poor devils.' Let us give the country well deserved good marks for that.

The Sovereign

At some point we have to ask who is behind running the country. Let us look at one of the key players, the sovereign, who holds the reigns and is responsible for everything. Under the terms of the *Grundgesetz*, literally translated as 'basic law', the German constitution, the people are the sovereign. As laid down in its Article 20 government has to do as they say. This places ultimate power over everything and final responsibility for how the country is governed clearly and unmistakably in the hands of the people.

In reality the Grundgesetz also says that the *Parteien*, the political parties, are to be *involved* in the process of law-making and governing the country. It may seem incredible, but such vague language is actually used in the context of something so important. Unfortunately the Grundgesetz says nothing about how they are to do this and has left the matter to be dealt with in *ordinary* legislation, by which, in due course, it was laid down that only such parties are to be represented in parliament at federal or state level that receive at least five per cent of the popular vote. It is usually maintained in government circles that this sprang from the belief that one should prevent splinter-groups from burdening the parliamentary process.

This looks harmless but the consequences are severe. It means: only such individuals can be elected into parliament, which are put up for election by a political party that receives at least five percent of the vote. In actual practice that means that you cannot run for a seat in parliament as an individual; you have to be nominated by one of the existing political parties. And that party has to receive five per cent of the vote or more. Thereby the parties decide who runs for parliament, not the voters, who have no say in the matter other than by letters to the press, complaining publicly or among friends or demonstrating in the streets.

All the voter can do is cast his or her vote for a party, which nominates the candidates. Half the seats in the Bundestag, the German federal parliament, are decided by direct vote, where the voter can elect candidates by name, which are put forward by the parties. The other half are decided on a percentage basis in accordance with the votes a party receives. If this sounds complicated that is precisely what it is. There is no grass-roots democracy and the voter has to trust the parties with regards to whom they put up for election. As a German citizen your sovereign rights boil down to your right to make crosses on the ballot paper that is put before you every so often, usually every four years - and that is it.

So: who is the sovereign, the people? You must be kidding: it is the parties. This is the root cause for at times endless party-wrangling and the forming of coalitions to secure a majority in parliament. Thereby the country gets a government, which is elected by parliament, not by the voter. Neither in the *Bundesregierung*, the federal government, nor one of the state governments, will you find one single office holder that was elected for this office by the people. They are every single one or as I am again and again prompted to say, the whole bloody lot of them, elected by their respective parliament. That parliament is made up of representatives nominated by the political parties, not by the people. The parties enter into coalition agreements to establish parliamentary majorities that will give them power, until such time as being replaced by another coalition, if parties change sides.

If membership in political parties is anything to go by take note that hardly more than two to two-and-a-half per cent of the population are political party members at federal or state level combined. And it is from within this segment of the population - save for rare exceptions - that governmental political office holders are put forward: a mere 2.5%, which in crude and naked figures means that something like 2,000,000 individuals out of the country's total population of some eighty million are involved in the organised political process as party members and office holders at state and country level.

In other words: those that are elected into government office come from within that tiny two-and-a-half per cent segment, put together at the whim and will of those running the political parties without any recourse to the general public. Anyone can set up a party, drum up support and get elected into one of the sixteen state parliaments or the federal Bundestag. That may look like the typical process whereby people like Ronald Reagan, Jimmy Carter, David Cameron or Barrack Obama pop up. The one distinct difference between these examples and Germany lies in the fact that the German public is not likely to go for public office holders unless they have come up through the rank and file of one of the parties, save for dramatic exceptions where a charismatic leader shoots to the top from out of nowhere, like . . . let me see . . . Hitler . . . scaremongering?

Let me ask again: who is the sovereign of the Federal Republic of Germany? That is a question of fundamental importance, seemingly totally ignored by the general public. People knowledgeable on constitutional matters say that in actual fact Germany is a party oligarchy, not a representative grass-roots democracy.

There is a whole lot in Germany that is in good stead. There are a number of things that are not. Running Germany's affairs is nobody's business but the Germans'. Germany is important, important to Europe, to the allies in NATO and to the world. For someone raised outside Germany certain things may be easier to detect and understand than for those whose personal history is solidly intertwined with that of the country.

There may be certain things about Germany and the Germans that will manifest themselves to you only if you can take a few steps back and put them into perspective with what you know from elsewhere. It appears that there may be something running through the country, based on history, traditions, experience and the nation's soul – I clearly believe that nations have souls – that introduces an element not found quite that readily elsewhere:

Angst.

I do not think that I need to translate the word, which to the best of my knowledge has found its way into the English language. There is an underlying element somewhere that you have to see, understand and weigh in its significance. It is something that has sprung from the collective experience of a nation that has gone through incredibly hard times and challenging situations. Perhaps it would be unfair to leave the Germans alone with that. Maybe, in the best sense of the word, they need a helping hand.

With their experience, history and culture the Germans of today are locked into a situation from which they may be unable to escape. But they have to. Someone or something is needed to cut through the Gordian Knot, brush away those unnecessary hindrances that prevent even a hint of a Grand Design from emerging, to overcome the many unnecessary little boundaries that have crept into daily life in Germany and the country's political system that prevent it from rising to the challenges of today and fulfil its true potential. There isn't really an awful lot wrong with the Germans. They simply deserve a better political system than the one they have.

Lingering Unease

Before an adequate leadership culture can establish itself in a country cultural awareness has to be in harmony with its emotional spirit, encompassing education, the arts and sciences and its moral orientation. The citizens have to see their hopes and aspirations reflected in the actions and objectives of their state to be able to support them whole heartedly. Having been blind and enthusiastic followers of a very evil regime, even if not openly declared, many Germans shied away from taking any stand at all and preferred to remain bystanders rather than integral parts of the new Germany. Thus a surprisingly large part of the population saw their relationship with Germany as a technicality rather than an affair of the heart, an attitude that has been passed on to this day in parts of the population.

Even after all that time for some Germans deep down inside there is the trauma of feeling a sense of shame over what the Nazis brought over the world. Others subconsciously seek reasons why they should not be ashamed. There is a hidden rift running through the country between those looking towards an emotionally unencumbered future for the country, having shaken off its dark history and those subconsciously reconciling with daily life that which is beyond their comprehension. Suspicions have never quite gone away of pockets of Nazi spirit nestled in somewhere in a somewhat darker corner of the nation's soul.

Rather than fudging over the matter, avoiding a clear stand one way or the other, it is perhaps time to think the matter through rationally. In the authoritarian state its proponents saw themselves as *good* and those against it as *bad*. For the ordinary citizen it was hard to draw a clear-cut line between uniformed Nazi-party members, Para-military units like the SA (short for Sturmabteilung, storm troopers, a uniformed arm of the party) and uniformed police. At that time anybody to the *left* of the Nazis and outside their immediate sphere was the enemy. That included all non-Arians, the Jewish population, everybody singled out as being ethnically non-German and all political affiliations with an orientation towards even the mildest form of socialism or outright communism.

After the end of Nazi rule an undercurrent remained to perpetuate that distinction. Although the Nazis were gone the dividing line continued to linger in some people's thinking. Newcomers to the country that did not quite look like what a *good* German should look like, predominantly migrant workers and many immigrants, were subconsciously added to some dark notion of *enemy*, rather than welcomed as an integral part of the population. This phenomenon continues to exist more widely among people with a lesser degree of education, but it is undeniably still there. Darwin or not, two thousand years of authoritarian society do not disappear overnight and continue to lead an ugly little existence in corners to which one normally pays no attention and which are not easily reached by the effects of education.

Sometimes it is little more than words, gestures, connotations, remarks . . . hard to pin down and even harder to remedy. If you can come up with a formula for eliminating prejudice that feeds on ignorance and jealousy, coupled with general lack of brightness, to avoid the word stupidity, you have a winner on your hands.

This is a problem that may lose significance with increased social advancement of the country but does constitute a lingering element of danger, should the country be pushed into a corner through unusual economic setbacks as a result of international or domestic turmoil. With parts of the East German population in conjunction with German unification the lingering problem was home-made. Eager to erase the memory of the communist past the West Germans dismantled all organisations that had in any way been connected with the state-run regime of the GDR. That meant *every* organisation from clubs, holiday institutions to recreational facilities and even kindergarten. This deprived East German youngsters of their social infrastructure, leaving them with too much time on their hands, nothing to do and no place to go. This undoubtedly created a void, part of which was eagerly absorbed by the newly emerging Neo-Nazis, which had surfaced from out of nowhere.

On more than one occasion police in Germany have been accused of leaning to the right, siding with Nazi sympathisers or outright Nazis. That is probably exaggerated. There may be a simple explanation that relates back to what we saw under the heading of 'Ordnung' and 'Ordnung machen', where these have a moralistic undertone. The police may subconsciously see uniformed marchers as an element of stability and their often somewhat rough looking opposite numbers as constituting a threat to that stability. This is highly irrational but it does seem to be there. The Nazis capitalised on this by almost always appearing in uniform. Of course the German police know the difference between Nazi hooligans and average citizens. Yet we have an element of irrationality that works against the state.

Outside known or suspected neo-Nazis there exists a segment of the population that may not be openly disposed towards siding with any Nazi activities. But like the sleepers in spy stories there may be a number of people of whom one does not know which way they will turn if push comes to shove. Assume dramatic economic or other setbacks or the like and a tight public safety situation and you may have a very unpleasant surprise on your hands.

We should beware.

There is one point that has somehow been created as a side-effect of dealing with the Nazis and their atrocities against the German Jewish population and that of other European countries that came under German domination. Before the Nazis we had citizens of these very countries that embraced Jewish faith and culture. After World War II we suddenly speak of Jews as if there existed a Jewish nationality, not to be confused with Israeli nationality. The German Jews were Germans of the Jewish faith, not citizens of another country. That order should be preserved, leaving it up to the individual as to whether he or she wanted to adopt Israeli citizenship, but as long as they were Germans they were members of the Jewish faith similar to German members of the Catholic or Protestant faith.

I suspect that there were forces promoting this injustice. It does not look like a coincidence. Somebody has been deliberately trying to create awareness that Jews are Jews and Germans are Germans, making the German Jews into foreigners in their own country.

I am still waiting for a public outcry.

The Long Road to Germany

One thing that is not widely known is the fact that in the course of history there were no fewer than three German Empires:

- The first one, called *The Holy Roman Empire of the German Nation*, sprang into life in the Middle Ages and was not a nation state but an agglomeration of political entities on what in due course was to become 'German soil'. It ultimately faded from memory with the end of the Napoleonic wars. Its *de facto* effectiveness ended with the Thirty-Year War, whilst it languished on as little more than an empty shell until being buried on the quiet as a consequence of a series of French victories in the Napoleonic Wars, climaxing in 1806, from which time onwards there exist no further *de jure* claims with regards to a German Empire, until the formation of the Second German Empire.

- We can be a bit more specific about the Second German Empire, called *Das deutsche Kaiserreich*, which was proclaimed by the Prussians at Versailles in France in 1871 and ended with the inglorious abdication in 1918 of the German Emperor. It lasted for a mere forty-seven (47) years. But what years! They saw Germany's rise to industrial super-power and its cataclysmic failure by defeat and surrender, marking the end of World War I.

- And then of course we had *Das Dritte Reich* commonly referred to as the Third German Empire, the life of which spanned a mere twelve (12) years from 1933 to 1945 and ended in the bloodiest and most cataclysmic World War yet.

Germany's road to statehood and international significance differs distinctly from that of its neighbouring countries. Whilst there exists widespread consensus that the roots of Europe draw on Greek/Roman culture and Christian/Jewish faith German cultural history has its roots in the dark, mythical Nordic/Germanic world with a distinctly different understanding of the roles of community, leadership and ancestry. They were embedded in a cultural sphere of their own, which was reflected in their understanding of religion, family and country, upholding the virtues of undivided loyalty – to the death if necessary – and total dedication to their leader, be he king or emperor. Although some may have longed for it, freedom was *never* an openly stated objective. Community, tribal or other affiliation ranked first and foremost and there existed a general preparedness to see things through in unquestioning faith and to the – at times bitter – end, whatever that would turn out to be.

Being a loose association of principalities, dukedoms, free cities and other autonomous entities, the Holy Roman Empire of the German Nation recognised an emperor as a worldly figure head. His authority in a wider sense was moral rather than physical. He balanced out the religious one, none less than the pope in his capacity as head of the Church. There was constant rivalry between state and Church. Save for on rare occasions this constellation hardly achieved the status of nation state. The proclamation of King Otto of the Saxons as Emperor of the Holy Roman Empire of The German Nation marks a rare highlight when everybody worth speaking of rallied behind him.

There was no clearly identifiable political structure. The empire constituted a forum in which the various Germanic entities conversed as particular events or circumstances may have demanded. In military terms there was no uniform command structure that could be called upon. With the end of the Thirty-Year-War in 1648 it ceased to play any significant part on the international stage. Reference to it - although not relating to any physical substance – lingered on until the Napoleonic wars and the defeat of German troops by the French under Napoleon in 1806, after which a consensus emerged 'that it was no longer there'. I have to put it as vaguely as that – there simply existed no 'German spirit' and hence there was no need to mark any beginning or end of it. In the German language the state of affairs that existed at the time is called 'Kleinstaaterei', which could be translated as a loose amalgamation of small states.

At the pre-nation stage in terms of international German significance in the greater hemisphere there still lingered a void. Any real power rested with the kingdom of Saxony, later joined by Prussia and still a bit later Bavaria, standing out above numerous other political entities, some mere free-cities, some being aristocrats' possessions of various sizes, until the Prussians' strong arm put an end to all that.

A country called Germany with clearly defined and internationally recognised boundaries, a nation state as such, did not come into existence until the proclamation of the German Empire by the German nobles assembled at Versailles, France, on 18 January 1871. On this day the various German political leaders were brought together by Prussia to celebrate victory over the French in a war rather deviously promoted by Prussian chancellor Bismarck so that 'all good German patriots' would rally behind Prussia and in a state of euphoria would proclaim the German Empire under Prussian leadership. From that day onwards the Prussian king became Emperor of Germany. Thereby he both *de jure* and *de facto* represented and owned what came to be known by historians as the Second German Empire. This was also the first national entity on German soil in which the chain of responsibilities and command extended into the most remote corners of its territory, top down from the emperor.

Those residing within the boundaries of the empire had switched their debt of allegiance to a larger entity, presided over by someone of higher rank. They continued to be subjects, whose rights and duties were now determined by the highest authority in the country, the emperor. Other than that not very much had changed for the population.

Whoever was at the head of the absolute state owned it and controlled the chain of command and responsibilities. That reduced the citizen or subject, rather, to paying taxes and otherwise 'shut up' as poet Heinrich Heine had put it. Thus, in the last instance, the subjects had to serve the emperor with all they had, including supporting any war effort and if need be give one's life.

It may be time to clear up a misunderstanding surrounding Austria and Germany or rather the various German states. Originally and ethnically they are all Germanic countries, except for political union. The First German Empire stood under the leadership of the Habsburg Dynasty. They were an original Germanic tribe equal to many others, albeit perhaps just a bit more equal. The German Emperors of the First Empire were Habsburgs, which in their latter days resided in Vienna. Over time the influence of the Emperor declined and that of other entities on German soil increased. There was rivalry and jealousy and many were content to see the Habsburgs squeezed out of German heartlands, that which constitutes today's Germany.

When the name Austria appeared it originally related to a German territory in a similar way as Wurttemberg, Saxony or Prussia, a late-comer. When it came to proclaiming the Second German Empire in 1871 there was considerable pressure to keep Austria out of it, successfully, and Austria channelled its energies in the direction of the Balkans, but it always retained the status of Empire. If things had gone a bit more smoothly we might perhaps see all of it as a greater Austria or a greater Germany, if they had managed to stay out of trouble and been content to managing within their more or less recognised national boundaries. Europe might have been a lot happier that way.

Alas, it was not to be.

It was a long road from Arminius Cheruscus in 09AD to 1871, proclaiming the German Empire. It took centuries for people to come to think of themselves as Germans rather than Prussians, Bavarians, Hanoverians or citizens or subjects of any other entity in Germanic lands.

Whose Country is it?

Over the course of the country's entire history German state philosophy knows only political entities of authoritarian to outright dictatorial persuasion, save for that tiny fifteen-year exception that we noted in the foregoing. Based on the tools readily available at the disposal of the state the powers that be imposed their will on the individual citizen as much as the entire political and social process, demanding unremitting obedience and respect for the state and the authority it represented. Therefore it should not come as a surprise that there existed no love between citizen and state. The citizen was awed by it, if not outright scared of the authorities, which reciprocated in a high-handed manner of impersonal coldness to outright contempt, making absolute demands. The great motivating force was fear, at times growing into *naked fear* of being threatened in one's very existence.

This has left its mark in a number of fields and can be summed up in the rather sad realisation that there existed in Germany no grass-roots democracy and no collective memory of any basic, unalienable rights, let alone equal rights for all. If there existed an understanding of 'freedom' and what it means this would have been quite different from what we mean today when we use the word. Freedom for the Germans has always somehow been intertwined with certain connotations, like freedom of movement or authority over one's economic life. The uprising in East Germany that was to lead to German unification certainly qualifies as a freedom movement. But it should not be overlooked that there was a strong economic motive, underlying the process, summed up in the slogan that reverberated through the streets at the time:

If the DM (the West German mark) does not come to us, we'll go to the DM.

Germans do not like this, if put to them in the form of a question, but it is my firm belief that the process of unification would have gone a different way if East Germany had been prospering rather than languishing on the brink of bankruptcy. Looking at Germany prompts a few questions about the Germans, their country and their state.

- If asked in the cold light of day: how would they describe their country?

- How do they see the relationship between citizen and state?

- What is their understanding of who owns the country, the physical entity and who the political one, the state?

- Who is *responsible* for the country, its well-being, its development and decisions that determine its fate?

For the entire period between the proclamation of the Second Empire in 1871 and the end of World War II in 1945 one finds practically nothing that would give rise to any hope that things evolved for the better. The end of Napoleonic rule over Germany had briefly nourished hopes of freedom. But those had been different freedoms that the various factions in the country craved:

- Ordinary citizens wanted personal freedom to develop their own, predominantly economic activities such as had been signalled by Napoleon's reforms and notably the introduction of the Code Civil.

- The aristocracy wanted restoration of their old, unlimited, God-given powers and rights.

- The students were on the whole conservative and rather chauvinistic, were often anti-Semitic with a distinct hatred for foreigners and nebulous visions of a Grand Germanic Empire, drawing on medieval history and proclaiming *teutsche* (ancient word for deutsch) virtues.

- Allusions to freedom related to freedom from foreign rule but not necessarily personal freedom as in *liberté, égalité, fraternité,* the maxims of the French Revolution.

After 1806 the blessings that Napoleon had brought through occupying vast parts of the country were quickly turned back. Power first reverted to the aristocracy and then the emperor. In 1848/9 a mild and widely unsupported democratic movement briefly sprang into existence, convened at Frankfurt's St Paul's Cathedral. The Prussian king was offered the crown of the German Emperor, which he rudely rejected as an insult, vilifying Democracy and its protagonists. In his estimation the God-given crown of the King of Prussia (which he held) towered high above Democracy. In 1871, soon after the failure of this movement the Prussians took things into their own hands to govern Germany in accordance with the laws determined by *blood and iron*, until and ending with Germany's defeat in World War I.

- The German Emperor had equated himself with Germany,

- The country and the Germans went along with that without protest, until it was too late.

- The same was repeated with Hitler and the dreadful consequences.

Unfortunately this sequence of events makes it dreadfully easy to answer the questions raised at the head of this chapter. Until victory of the Allies in Germany in May 1945 it was crystal-clear that the Germans were subjects of the Empire or Reich, respectively, and that all powers, rights and privileges were vested in Emperor or Hitler, respectively, who thereby also owned state and country. Unbelievably their powers were unlimited, absolute and irreversible. That sadly answers the question as to who up to 1945 owned Germany.

For the time after 1945 things are not really all that clear. The relics of authoritarian rule moved away only too reluctantly, some still hanging on today. It seems like a miracle as consensus took hold in the country that the people are citizens, not subjects, endowed with certain unalienable rights. But it will still take some time. Rome wasn't built in a day. I like to believe that the Germans are getting there but they have to remain vigilant as not all ghosts from the past have been terminally defeated.

There was a slow and steady progression from tribal culture to elements of statehood. In what concerns our basic and fundamental understanding we can be brief: throughout German history none of the intermediate stages of national evolution got anywhere near Democracy.

Even the German/Prussian philosophies of *Aufklärung*, enlightenment, and *Idealismus*, idealism, kept well away from what was happening on the cultural scene in the rest of Europe as did the arts, literature and music. German Romanticism in poetry, Bach's religious devotion and Wagner's heavy emotions in music are all specifically German or Germanic, if you prefer.

Hitler would not have been able to do it alone. He relied on followers, some blind, some cunning, some unbelievably stupid but one element never had a decisive say: the people, their only means of expression being enthusiastic, loud public support at party-rallies. They failed to resist in time and had to bear the consequences to the end.

The principle of authoritarian rule infuses the individual with the notion that his own existence is worthless unless dedicated to a 'higher' cause, over which he has absolutely no control. As the avenue of citizenship is limited to following orders, creativity goes into striving for perfection in other fields.

In the absence of meaningful, constructive outlets for their energies the Germans saw only one choice: no matter what you do, be good at it if not the best. Thus, sadly, the Germans' striving for perfection is perhaps the root cause for their preparedness to charge ahead regardless without the critical distance to challenge the validity of something, once embarked upon. This may enable them to perform great deeds but equally become engulfed in great evil, unable to fathom things out properly.

Looking for a date to signify the coming about of a new Germany I propose 23 May 1949, the date on which in a constitutional assembly the German states that had emerged after the end of the war adopted and signed the Grundgesetz, which was to be the constitution of the country and marked the formation of the Federal Republic of Germany. This is also the country's first open adoption of Democracy as its core philosophy.

The Individual and the State

The relationship between the Germans and their state is different from that of any other country. This seemingly provocative statement implies a privileged situation. That is not the intention. Different here means simply that it is characterised by certain features that are not to be found elsewhere to the same extent or with the same intensity. Generalisations invite protest. The following may be over-simplified but the intention is to bring out something specific: the *cultural quality* of the relationship between citizen and state. Above and beyond moral or emotional quality the cultural aspect encompasses all facets of what unites citizens with and puts them apart from their state, which is not limited to arts and crafts or historical heritage.

I am tempted to draw on my professional background when it comes to explaining *culture* in the sense in that I want to use the word in this context. When aeronautical engineers – admittedly somewhat pompously - speak of a *Boeing* or an *Airbus culture* they refer to something that everybody in the industry understands: Boeing culture means doing something in a way that is characteristic for Boeing, like where you place things, how you connect them and how they are to be operated and maintained. A pilot who has come up through a Boeing culture when confronted with another Boeing aircraft from the one he last flew will find the position of things and how to handle them without the need for much explaining. The same goes for Airbus. Perhaps cultural quality can be related to that. Every country and every society has a specific culture in the sense that they have a particular way of seeing and doing things.

For openers let me choose at random such a simple thing as crossing a street. In London you may walk across the street on a red light if it is safe to do so and that is your choice. In Berlin you get a ticket regardless of the traffic situation if there is a policeman on hand who sees it. That means that in London the prevailing street-crossing-culture will use the 'perceived-walking-safety-aspect', what you see and what you make of it, as your decision-making criteria, whilst in Berlin you have to follow the letter of the law, regardless of the actual traffic situation. You may get away with it with a guilty conscience and mothers with small children will give you disapproving stares for setting a bad example, but things may come to a head if a policeman is there to observe the scene and he may then be required by law to book you.

So the Germans as per this example have rules and the English do not?

Wrong! The English certainly do. They are masters at rules-and-regulations. To bring it to the point: in England you obey the rules and that is an absolute must. The difference between England and Germany lies in the fact that in England the rules are unwritten, same as the country has a constitution that does not exist in writing and there exists no comprehensive book of laws in print-form. It is all in the mind, verbal. It is 'up in the air', in a manner of speaking, embedded in the heart and soul of society. Same as our understanding of life evolves in an ongoing way, so does the concept that the English have of rules-and-regulations, updating itself in a mysterious, unspoken way. When it comes to the crunch, you observe and you decide, drawing guidance from your heart and soul.

The Germans will have none of that. They want something that stands above a spur-of-the-moment interpretation, which can be held up as a yardstick for everybody. Hence there has to be a law that applies to everybody and is fool-proof, there for all to see, that tells you when you may cross a street. It will stand in court in the form of tangible evidence, given by the policeman who saw you crossing the street on a red light, should you dispute it. Never mind the traffic situation. If you want to have rules that are legally enforceable you have to remove the possibility for human error and base your judgment on objectively recognisable evidence, there for everyone to see, record – if necessary – and preserve in the form of photographic records. Shooting at sparrows with cannons? The Germans do not think so, but take this matter quite seriously. Their attention focuses entirely on the legal aspect, not the content matter, the traffic situation that prevailed as and when the alleged breach of law occurred.

To broaden the scope let us make some cursory comparisons between three countries, which are distinctly different from one another in their basic patterns but convey the impression to the unsuspecting observer that they all function equally well and seemingly all in the same way. Having already selected England and Germany let me add France, another one of the 'big three'. My reference to England rather than the United Kingdom or Great Britain is deliberate: That which is typical and specific for the UK in this particular context is found in the English. Let us leave aside for the time being the Welsh, Scots or Irish to simplify the situation. That way we do not have to be concerned with their peculiarities and can focus on what traditionally over the centuries stood out for England as one of the dominant world powers. This, in a nutshell, is the long and the short of the relationship in the three countries between individuals and their state:

- The English treat their state with respect and so vice-versa does the state with regards to the individual

- The French love it with heart and soul, are proud of it, and think of it as part of their extended family

- The Germans view it with a mixture of fear and reverence, prepared to give it their all-and-everything but also making absolute demands

The attitude of the English is pragmatic and mature. Looking back on a thousand-year history of statehood both sides have had enough time and opportunity to learn and understand how far either side can go and what they are likely to get away with. Therefore there is little to no contention in defining the respective role. In history along the way there were such milestones as the Magna Charta and the Bill of Rights and whatever contention there may have been has burnt out so that there are no unresolved issues between state and individual.

France has enjoyed statehood for practically as long as England. During the earlier phases of the monarchy there existed *co-habitation* between king, aristocracy and common people. The expression has come back into fashion as of late. It describes very well what characterises French outlook on life, reflected in what we sum-up as *laisser-faire* and *savoir-vivre:* mind your own business and enjoy life. It may be a fortunate co-incidence that much of the country lies in a sunny climate-zone, whilst the absence of a distinct division over religious issues must have helped. The Protestant Huguenots at the time were quickly ushered out of the country, often by less than friendly means and incidentally came to be such a marvellously positive influence in Prussia or their other respective new home countries, to which many of them escaped from harsh oppression in France. This compares in no way to the disruptive effect of the Reformation in Germany and its consequences, the upheaval brought over the country by The Thirty-Year-War.

I hesitated whether I should bring in wine, women and song to describe a dominant feature of French culture, as that may be more appropriately reserved for the Italians. But it is clear that there must at least be tacit understanding that the different parties making up society respect one another and their niches, each giving the other space to breathe. I would sum up that attitude in that in France you would not start a conflict, let alone a war, during their generously timed lunch-breaks.

The relationship between state and individual is marked by passion, which can go two ways: normally it is love, but in the run-up to the French Revolution, its tumultuous duration and the aftermath things erupted in hate. This was the kind of hate that you can experience only after you have loved, before things turned bad. Thus, the effects were not lasting and quickly overcome, like in a good family quarrel.

The French came out of the Revolution and the Napoleonic period that followed with many a good thing to show for it, including devolution, the complete separation of state and church, a noteworthy piece of law in the form of the *Code Napoléon*, later evolved into the *Code Civil* and the fact that they enshrined once and for all the maxims of *liberté, fraternité, égalité*.

To help us not to forget this they built the Statue of Liberty and shipped it out to America, where it stands to this day to greet you as you enter New York Harbor. Seeing it for the first time can be a heart-warming sight and convey deep feelings and lasting memories. The French always struck me as having a natural understanding of that which stands out in life above and beyond everyday routine. I guess it's like their cooking, something to do with spices.

We have already been alerted to expect something quite different when it comes to slotting in the Germans. The characteristics of their relationship between state and individual are what — with a bit of luck — can evolve, if a basically industrious and intelligent tribe wants to make the best of getting ahead in life in the limited space granted between the heavy hand of state supremacy, interspersed with — in its better moments - benevolent tyranny. Germany's society evolved in an austere climate that although not religious *per se* draws on ingrained qualities of centuries of religious teachings and demands.

The forces shaping the mindset of the individual were, on the one hand, the Church, originally the one and only Christian Church. This held true up to 31 October 1517. On that day Martin Luther nailed his ninety-five theses of dissent to the portal of the chapel of Wittenberg Castle. Thereby he split the Church in two and from this moment onwards we refer to it as the Catholic and the Protestant Church. Neither of the two shades of Christianity was overly concerned with the individual rights of the ordinary person as opposed to his or her respective duties and obligations.

The other dominant force were the rulers of the day, be they emperor, king or noblemen. Of these the Protestant part, in particular the Prussian kings, reached out one step further: they wanted to make rights and obligations applicable to and enforceable for all, driven by a somewhat puritan sense of justice. This included, if need be, making them binding on the king himself and the aristocracy — and there is evidence on record to that effect.

The consequence of this was rigidity. Once something existed in writing in the form of laws, decrees, regulations or the like things had a tendency to become static. Matters that had been passed into law stayed, to preserve the status-quo, even until after the matter which they had sought to address had either gone away or been dealt with otherwise. Bureaucracy crept into the relationship of the common man or woman and those above them, to play a steadily increasing part in daily life.

By sheer co-incidence Charles Darwin recently featured prominently in the media for having alerted the world to the principle of evolution, summarised and climaxing in his findings about the survival of the fittest. Thereby it is an undeniable fact that species either evolve or perish. Darwin started out with plants and birds, but things did not end there. The fundamental laws of Nature apply to all and every species on this earth. In today's world the principle of evolution has become an accepted and undisputed piece of science, save for some less visited parts of the United States, where people steadfastly hold on to the principles of creationism.

To those, fewer in number, the Germans may appear as a species that was created the way it is and always has been. The rest of us may be inclined to accept the principle that same as any other species the Germans were shaped by the forces that acted on them, threatening or enhancing their chance of survival. Let us briefly recall the survival strategies that were a must if it was your fate to live, survive and succeed in Germany:

- Practice a trade, the arts or commerce, be good at it and pay your taxes

- Don't come to the attention of those above you unless the news is good

- And do what those above you demand of you, enthusiastically and without complaining

This is an almost classical survival strategy, if you emerge from centuries of not merely social but often physical pressure, in particular the might of the state that gave you little to no choice. Eminent thinkers like famous poet Heinrich Heine had to flee the country to France, wanted by the Prussian police for being an outspoken, free thinker; national poet celebrate Friedrich Schiller was a fugitive from politically motivated justice as was composer Richard Wagner and Johann Sebastian Bach, the highly respected and much revered composer, did time in jail for wanting to terminate his employment contract. Such circumstances of life were bound to generate a certain form of opportunism, driven by the humanly understandable desire to brighten up your prospects in life, in particular stay out of jail and in some cases merely - alive.

The political environment may have made little to no difference if you were a farm-hand or a labourer, but its at times suffocating effects were inescapable, the higher your position in the society in which you wanted to make a success of things. Some chose to lie low, like scientist Galileo, who left his native country to escape the pressure. Many in Europe went to America, where they were to become a highly creative and productive element, contributing their talents to fuelling American Independence.

By contrast, in Germany your chances of doing your own thing and succeeding were quite limited, if you were not one of the privileged few. So why didn't the Germans rebel against this oppression like the French, who abandoned all respect for traditions and accepted roles of the various parts of society and simply went ahead to chop off the heads of all those of whom they thought that they stood in the way of reform, on occasion throwing in a few innocent bystanders? Strange as this may seem, the Germans may at the time have shied away from bloodshed on a scale that would have made a difference.

Christianisation had prospered on streams of blood. The Thirty-Year-War was a bloody way to settle the differences between opposing sides of the religious argument. The Inquisition was still fresh on people's minds, warring factions like Napoleon, conquering or roaming the country, showed little respect for people's sensitivities. Hence the average person residing on German soil in any one of the many extant political entities was all but spoiling for a bloody revolution. On top of that the aristocracy up into the highest ranks preferred to pamper the citizens, as long as they did what was expected of them, by which I would like to re-direct your attention to what I said a little earlier:

Opportunism enhanced your chances of survival, taking a liberal stand was a killer.

There is perhaps one decisive element that makes Germany stand apart from any other European country. The Germanic dark and joyless heritage must have done a lot to drive the common man or woman right into the arms of its equally dark and joyless successor, the Church. In its initial stages it was little more than an instrument for subjugating people, bringing them to heel and thereby consolidating the worldly powers, which in turn displayed gratitude and helped to consolidate the Church.

If I had to single out significant elements that almost unavoidably settled the Germans on the course that they were to follow, in due course, up to and including World Wars I and II, Hitler, the Holocaust and all that goes with it, I would name:

- The legacy of dark Germanic heritage

- Unfortunate events in early history that kept Germania apart from the rest of Europe

- The Reformation of the Church and Martin Luther's teachings of its being God-given

- The ensuing upheavals, like The Thirty-Year War

- And the emergence of Prussia, first as a dukedom, followed by kingdom and followed by becoming the nucleus of the German Empire of Kaiser Wilhelm

I have heard otherwise sensible people say that composer Richard Wagner was a Nazi. That is of course nonsense. He may have had ideas that later other people were also having but Wagner was there first, thinking whatever he did or did not think. The Nazis usurped and misappropriated his music.

Martin Luther certainly cannot be held responsible for anything that happened five hundred years after his time. The fateful connection here lies in the fact that he endorsed authoritarian rule as God-given: *Es gibt keine Obrigkeit ohne von Gott*, was the relevant piece of gospel, meaning quite literally that all and any authority is God-given. The pillars of society in the Protestant parts of Germany pounced on this as their life-blood, including the King of Prussia.

By virtue of this, politics and religion were intertwined to the point that for the common person there existed no distinguishing morale. Obeying your ruler was no more and no less than abiding by the will of God. Those who might have rebelled on political grounds were prevented by their faith from taking action or, more profanely, the fear of God. To the ordinary common person the line of demarcation between church and state became increasingly blurred to the point that people did not really distinguish between the two, endowing the latter with an aura of standing above all else. This *junctim* simply happened as an element of historical evolution and caught hold even of such people that were not religious at heart.

Many Germans today are as open to the world, as enlightened and as liberated as people elsewhere. They care about their country and they want it to succeed and prosper. The constraints imposed by the existing political and sociological environment drive them to realise that it is *Realpolitik* that gets you ahead in life rather than the will to make significant reforms. You abide by what is there and try to make the best of it. You can call this opportunism, if you like, but it is really a survival strategy that has evolved over the centuries. Thus, these are our findings, returning to our three examples:

- The English continue to do what they are good at, being pragmatic and in many ways politically mature

- The French continue to be as French as ever

- And the Germans continue to do what they have been doing ever since the end of World War II and the early days of the Bundesrepublik: they accept the prevailing form and framework, almost as if it were God-given.

And all that, in a nutshell, is the reason why you should not cross streets on a red light when in Germany, at least not as long as there is a policeman anywhere near.

From Ruins to German Unification

After the cessation of hostilities between Germany and the Allies, climaxing in Germany's unconditional surrender on 08 May 1945, there followed a period of several months, during which the victors were faced with the daunting task of structuring and initiating the re-birth of the country that had caused so much hardship, damage and pain. One of the first priorities was separating potential friends from foes and quite literally gearing things up again, having suddenly been saddled with ensuring the survival of the former enemy, the Germans. The losers had no choice but to try and sort themselves out and survive as best they could, some embittered with crushed egos, the majority with relief that the Nazi nightmare was over and hope in their hearts of better times to come.

A rift in the relationship was beginning to take hold between the Western Allies on the one hand, which were primarily the United States, Great Britain and France, and the Soviet Union, on the other, together the victors. Germany was now divided into four occupation zones, of which the American, British and French zones taken together formed a contiguous entity that was eventually to become the Federal Republic of Germany, short FRG or BRD – the German way and the Russian one, the German Democratic Republic, short DDR in their language culture or GDR the English way.

But before it could come to that basic living essentials had to be restored like water supply, sewerage, gas, electricity and the first rudiments of a public transport system of trains, busses and streetcars, all this in an environment of mountains of debris from damaged or destroyed buildings and structures. Most of the bridges across the rivers Rhine, Weser, Elbe and Danube had been knocked out. The entire infrastructure had been badly damaged due to extensive aerial bombing and on-the-ground fighting. Resistance by the German armed forces had been particularly tenacious in the path of the advancing Red Army and war damage was severe in some areas.

To the east of a demarcation line constituted by the rivers Oder and Neisse all former parts of Germany had to be given up and were annexed unilaterally as compensation for war damages: the northern half of East Prussia with its principal city of Koenigsberg, the birthplace of philosopher Immanuel Kant, by the Soviet Union and its southern half and the former German provinces of West Prussia, Silesia and parts of Pomerania by Poland. Some three million German inhabitants of these territories had fled to the West, never to return to their respective home countries.

The refugees had arrived with barely more than they could carry in their hands, most of the East and West Prussians by ship across the Baltic Sea. They all needed shelter and housing, food and clothing, as did all the many people in the West whose houses had been destroyed by bombing. Coping with an unprecedented exodus and resettling such large numbers of people was a formidable task, given the severely damaged infrastructure of what was left of Germany. In retrospect this has to go down in history as a major accomplishment of the Germans, only made possible through very generous help from the Allies, not to forget the American Marshall Plan.

The political and administrative establishment of the country had been compromised by its past under the Nazis. The Allies, out of sheer necessity and initially very reluctantly, gradually brought back some people from the previous administration, trying to keep out known Nazis and those under suspicion of having been involved in war crimes. For sheer lack of a sufficient number of suitable people this became increasingly difficult when restoring general administrative services, the police, the judicial and education. Despite strenuous efforts many a rotten apple slipped through, sowing the seeds of an undercurrent of discontent that sweltered over the years until erupting in the student revolts of 1968, when primarily younger people wanted to clean up what their parents had failed to finish.

Right from the outset those Germans that were to rise to play a part in future political life came out in favour of a federal system of states that were to some extent defined arbitrarily, not really reflecting former political entities. On the whole names were retained, save for Prussia, which was thought to have been at the heart of German militarism and many an unappealing feature of the Third Reich. Therefore the name Prussia and anything with a Prussian connotation was purged from future political life of the Federal Republic.

In 1948/9 a system of states, called Bundesländer, was reinstated and first parliamentary elections were held under the auspices of the Western Allies. There emerged in due course ten states, comprising the British, American and French occupation zones and Berlin, which had been carved up into the three Western sectors of the Western Allies and East Berlin under Soviet control.

By the middle of 1948 the Western Allies had decided that the moment had arrived to reinstate some form of German statehood. On 01 September 1948 *der Parlamentarische Rat,* the Parliamentary Council, was convened in Bonn, which had as its sole task the working out and agreeing of the country's future constitution. This was prepared in a series of consultations between eminent Germans, who had stayed above reproach, and representatives of the Allies. Instead of *Verfassung,* which means constitution, the document was called *Grundgesetz,* literally Basic Law. The choice of wording reflected the temporary nature of the document that was produced on the notion that the division of Germany into East and West was merely temporary.

As the Soviets had refused to become involved in this exercise the future Fathers and Mothers of the Grundgesetz, as they were to be called, sought to write up their draft in such a way that there would be nothing that could obstruct German unification at some point in the future. They were sixty-one men and four women, representing the Western occupation zones and five non-voting members, representing the Western sectors of Berlin. In drafting the Grundgesetz they went out of their way to avoid anything that could possibly lead to a repetition of the events that brought down the Weimar Republic. Needless to say that the Western Allies looked over their shoulders to ensure that the final draft would be to their satisfaction.

On 23 May 1949 the Grundgesetz was signed by the principal representatives of the states and proclaimed as the supreme law of the new Federal Republic of Germany. This also marks the birth of the new Germany. There were two important *technicalities,* both of which are connected with Konrad Adenauer, here defining technicality as an initial decision that then was to set the course of everything else.

- Number one: Adenauer was elected to become the first Bundeskanzler, effectively the prime minister of the new country.

- Number two: the city of Bonn, of which Konrad Adenauer had been the mayor, was chosen as the new German capital.

Much as some said that this reeked of favouritism it had convincing logic to it: Bonn had not suffered much war damage and its urban infrastructure had remained intact. Adenauer knew the place like his hip pocket, having been responsible for running it for a number of years as mayor and it was small enough to dispel any concerns that the rest of the world might have about any future German delusions of grandeur. The only competitor had been Frankfurt. Given the smooth start of German political life emanating from it, opting in favour of Bonn turned out to have been a wise decision.

With the invaluable benefit of hindsight we can now say that those masterminding German Unification forty years later, in 1990, after the Iron Curtain and with it the Berlin Wall had come down, must have lost sight of this original intention or chosen to ignore it. Much as that would have been the perfect opportunity to have a close look at the Grundgesetz and give it a good shake-up nothing of the sort was done. Constitutional reform in conjunction with German Unification consisted of little more than adding the names of what were to become the five new eastern states and check and adjust any wording in conjunction therewith.

For the East Germans the only choice was to join, no ifs and buts. There was *der Einigungsvertrag*, the Unification Agreement, which dealt with technicalities. What received precious little to no attention was the intellectual and moral content of what was entailed in abolishing a formerly sovereign state, the German Democratic Republic, although the West Germans had never formally recognised it as such. Thus the territory of the former GDR or German Democratic Republic was inducted in an extant country. The choice for the East Germans was little more than unilateral acceptance. In a material sense the West Germans performed admirably. In what concerned the heart and soul of the matter one might have done things differently

Looking for a State Philosophy

Having thus set the scene for the emergence of a new country called Germany it is high time to go back to first steps and look at the underlying state philosophy that motivates it, inspires its people and emits a message to the outside world. The people selected to draft the Grundgesetz were politically above reproach, of personal integrity, but had only a rather narrow choice of guidance from history. The only example of democratic rule in Germany was the Weimar Republic, which had lasted for a mere decade-and-a-half in the wake of World War I and apparently did not serve as a source of inspiration. The Allies monitoring the process were primarily concerned with safeguarding against a repetition of the Nazi horrors. Apparently nobody checked it against some of the salient provisions of the American Constitution that had become such a powerful, well proven and admirable document, so that one or two of the shortcomings of the Grundgesetz slipped through the draft stage undetected.

Same as with any company that sets its sights on being successful, a country needs a vision, a philosophy that inspires its people and fills them with the conviction of being in the right place, doing the right thing. The following examples encompass the range of alternative choices, even extremes, from which the successful philosophy would emerge or be composed, blending together the good and avoiding the bad, going through what seemed like a comprehensive choice of options. With utter simplification they were the following:

- The Ideal State

- Authoritarian Rule

- Laisser-Faire

- The Conservative State Philosophy and

- The Social Market Economy

Appearances are that in today's Germany none of these has gained the upper hand but the last one, which after World War II emerged as decisive in shaping the future of the country, certainly helped to get it going again and give it a solid foundation, for as long as that lasted.

Here they are in a broad overview, respectively.

The Ideal State

Duly elected by the citizens the Chancellor, relying on a government of un-selfish helpers, dedicated to making any sacrifice towards the furtherance of the nation, conscientiously and diligently manages its affairs, serving faith-fully and to the best of his ability as do those called into government office. Regardless of their own benefits and welfare it is their principal concern that the citizens may enjoy a life in peace, the blessings and fruits of their work in a harmonious social, political and natural environment, sheltered by a sympathetic system of social security and healthcare, enabling them to bene-fit from the fruits of their working life in tranquillity and harmony for as long as they may live.

Wow! – Paradise! Is it the obligation of government to create paradise on earth for the citizen? We may doubt that. Such an expectation would go way beyond that which any government can deliver at the best of times.

The Ideal State served as little more than a vision. Touched upon were two extremes and something 'in-the-middle', including notably that which lay behind people in the form of the Empire and the Third Reich.

Authoritarian Rule

Highest legal and moral priority entrusted into the hands of the state and those in whom its authority is vested is the assurance of its continued exist-ence and that of those overseeing its affairs so that in turn it may shelter the citizens and safeguard their interests.

The state protects the national boundaries and carries the responsibility within and without for the integrity of the national society and economy, in which the citizens may pursue their legitimate interests in the framework of a well ordered social and economic environment, guided, overseen by and answerable to the state.

In return the citizens are obliged to dedicate their economic commitment to the state, paying their taxes and making available to it that which it may require in the furtherance of its well-being and the pursuit of its interests at the sole discretion of its leaders. Thereby the furtherance of the common good takes precedence over that of the individual.

The state deems itself to be the defender of occidental, Christian ideals and values and demands the unlimited, total commitment of its citizens to the furtherance of its goals, including the preparedness to fulfil military service if the state, at its sole discretion, engages in acts of national defence or war.

These were pretty much the guidelines of the Empire of Kaiser Wilhelm. The Weimar Republic did not make a big splash and there was not a noteworthy change to these maxims. Weimar had been a hastily instituted system that would have needed more time to evolve into a true democracy.

When the Nazis were first given power legally and then grabbed the rest of it the fundamental principles as outlined for the Totalitarian State did not change much. If anything, the rights of the citizen were reduced to paying taxes, supporting the Nazis and the war effort and otherwise keeping quiet.

The countries of the Soviet Bloc, in particular the GDR, pretty much fell into the same category, with little to no room for freedom of the individual as we know it in a democratic state. Hence they hardly provided any shining examples of successful democracies, which could have served as guidance when drawing up the Grundgesetz for the new Germany.

Here now is the opposite, in some ways, of Authoritarian Rule, the philosophy of Laisser-Faire, which could have become the new philosophy of an emerging Germany:

Laisser-Faire

Supreme principle is the freedom of the individual, limited only by any indispensable, fundamental and essential necessities such as may be required so that the state may fulfil its obligations with regards to maintaining its integrity and essential institutions and services, while providing a safe and well-ordered environment, in which the citizens may pursue their endeavours.

The state grants the citizens total and unrestricted freedom in their personal and private lives as well as in the conduct of business above and beyond concerns of public safety and integrity of the state's institutions. Subject to stringent overseeing by their duly elected representatives the citizens agree to the payment of any appropriate and necessary taxation. In return for the freedoms granted by the state the citizens accept the sole responsibility for making appropriate provisions at their own cost in respect of unemployment, healthcare and old age. Any obligations in respect of the defence of

The principle of Laisser-Faire in many of its aspects is not very far away from unbridled capitalism and some of its salient features cannot be implemented in a modern state as they fall short of general public acceptance.

The Conservative State Philosophy

The Conservative state philosophy is a form of Laisser-Faire that seeks to reconcile certain aspects of public concern with the demands for unlimited freedom of the individual under the heading of: as much state as necessary but as little state interference as possible. The state is to focus on its essential tasks, be good at it, and otherwise leave matters in the hands of the citizens. Other than that it incorporates the principles of Laisser-Faire.

Let us leave aside Socialism, which places any concern for the welfare of the citizens in the hands of the state and Communism, which goes one step further, abolishing private property and practically any freedom of choice by the citizens. Neither of the two came under discussion in conjunction with the Grundgesetz as being too extreme with the inherent risk of slipping back into totalitarian rule, from which Germany had just been salvaged.

Although neither mentioned in its context nor specifically written into any clauses of the Grundgesetz, the state philosophy that emerged as guidance for drafting the new constitution was defined as the maxims of the Social Market Economy, in German *Soziale Marktwirtschaft*, which seeks to establish a fair and equitable basis in which all differences that may arise between different groups or segments of the population are reconciled with state integrity and over-all soundness:

The Social Market Economy

The Social Market Economy seeks to establish and maintain a fair and healthy balance between the legitimate and unalienable rights of the state and its individual citizens, between the economically more and the less well-endowed, the sexes and the generations, while preserving the continued existence and well-being of the state. Above and beyond the citizens' commitment to respecting social and economic balance the state will safeguard their personal, political and economic freedom and enhance free enterprise.

The citizens enable the state to levy all and any taxation that it may need to assure its continued existence and that of its institutions. In addition the state may raise and allocate appropriate public funding, called Umvertei-

lung, re-distribution in English, to ensure the creation and maintenance of a fair and healthy balance between the economically more and the less well-endowed, the sexes and the generations. Thereby the state is enabled to create and maintain a social safety net, ein soziales Netz, which will provide a bottom line in respect of the welfare of its citizens.

Broadly speaking the Social Market Economy is a cross between the Authoritarian model and Laisser-Faire, bordering on Capitalism, into which a component of social balance is infused; in other words:

Do what you can get away with, as long as enough remains to create a sound balance between the rich and the poor, men and women and the young and the old.

The Soziale Marktwirtschaft came to be one of the cornerstones of Germany's re-emergence as an economically strong, politically stable country. A number of measures introduced under that heading served to create a sound economic balance for a wide spectrum of the population. It did not impoverish anybody nor did it make anybody unduly rich. But its result was the creation of widespread purchasing power in the hands of many, employment for most if not all and a general fuelling of the economy. High productivity and low labour costs meant swift increases in Germany's GDP, washing lots and lots of tax money into government coffers.

There were other factors that worked in favour of a swift economic and thereby also political re-emergence of Germany. After the war years the population was hungry for modest economic success and thus prepared to work hard. There was almost unlimited demand for the goods produced in Germany on a reasonably open and unrestricted market. On top of that the American Marshall Plan brought a capital infusion to start up production and demand not merely in Germany but in a number of European countries.

There was an unexpected windfall from the Korean War, which saw Germany readily available and in a position to supply its particular needs when most other countries that would otherwise have played a significant part were engulfed in problems of their own, whilst Germany in addition to almost all other things had also been freed from many of its traditional obligations and was ready to pounce on the situation.

The State Philosophy of the Social Market Economy was an admirable piece of prudent foresight, which helped to create that base of stability and elementary wealth creation that was to manifest itself in the much admired *Wirtschaftswunder*, the German Economic Miracle. For about ten to fifteen years, from the 1950s onwards, it was the determining force affecting Germany's economy, until other forces gained the upper hand and outperformed it.

Economy and Continuity

When we look at some of the major countries in Europe against the background of their history, say the United Kingdom and France, we see continuity. Doing so for Germany since the nation state was founded in 1871 we see a country vigorously plodding on over two periods, each of which abruptly ended in chaos that wiped out the accrued achievements: the first one of forty-seven, the second of twenty-seven years, both periods ending in the cataclysmic turmoil of a world war that Germany started and lost.

So much for track record.

For Germany there exists no continuity on which you can build a picture based on proven past experience that you can project into the future. Today's Germany is the country that the Allies of World War II liberated from Nazi rule and which we have to judge on the strengths and weaknesses of its accomplishments since then - albeit with the country's history in the back of one's mind wherever that may be relevant.

My concern is the new Germany, a new country, shaking off the constraints imposed by the past, to be the first national entity on German soil that is enjoying democratic rule – the first ever in some two thousand years from the fateful days of Arminius Cheruscus, whose military exploits opened up the route for two thousand years of authoritarian rule over the country. So we are looking at a recent and brief period in history, coming up to sixty years from the collapse of Nazi Germany in 1945 to today . . . . and counting.

Thus, while Britain and France can look back on about thirty and the United States on eight generations of meaningful continuity in history, the Germany that we are concerned with looks back on a mere two generations, making that an infant country. To compound the irony inherent in this I have to admit that I am older than the Federal Republic, for whatever that is worth: I saw it come and I do not want to have to see it go, falling by the wayside. Such language introduces a dramatic undertone and implies that I am motivated by a sense of danger, impending danger for Germany as a country, its people and those affected by it, Europe and the

World. Dramatic as that may sound I cannot see anything happening in and with Germany on a major scale that does not have serious and far reaching repercussions for the rest of the world. Everything is now connected with everything else to such an extent that none of the major countries and economies can be seen in isolation. For better or worse they have all become part of the grand total of global interdependence, which determines stability and peace.

Let us reassure ourselves why we should not be alarmed: the German economy is the proverbial rock in a stormy sea, standing head and shoulders above all those countries that have to struggle to balance the books, among them Greece, at times referred to as the cradle of Democracy, Portugal and Spain, steeped in culture and tradition, Italy, in many ways the mother of European civilisation and not to forget little Iceland out in the North Atlantic, which despite turbulent elements in its past has an impressive history of Democracy. The United States was good for giving Germany a fresh start after the disastrous Nazi period and - by the way — has since then been good for quite a few percentage points on Germany's export statistics.

They are all modern countries with a sophisticated, intelligent and educated population. Their national economies all have a problem to make ends meet, some more, some less and why? There may be a number of contributing causes but one of them is undeniably something that was only made possible through the breathtaking advancement of our society and economy: the spectre of consumerism that gripped people, wanting all those lovely things that our modern industry can produce and supply.

And who figured prominently among those that fuelled this consumerism and served enthusiastically to supply the lovely goods that so many people just could not live without? Might not this be where the self-declared *Exportweltmeister*, the world champion of exports, may have a case to answer, the makers, suppliers and exporters of luxury cars and all those attributes of affluence? On the one hand we have the rock in the stormy sea, the world champion of exporting industries and on the other the consumers in a multitude of countries, without which the makers and producers would have nothing to make, produce and export.

What will happen if economies cool down, for whatever reasons? In the sunny countries around the Mediterranean they will do what they have always done: protest, smash up a few police cars, shake their fists and then sit down over an espresso, an ouzo, a pastis or a glass of their delicious local wine, talk among themselves and think. After they have let off steam they will come to the sobering conclusion that it is up to them to sort themselves out. It will be neither quick nor easy. They will muddle through, moan and groan and then fall back on their own devices and rebuild their environment with what is at their disposal and readily available. In the long run they will discover that there are a lot of things that they do not really need and quite a few that they do not have to buy abroad. After initial turmoil and upheaval they will come out a little bit healthier than they were before and they will gear up to face the future, perhaps at a somewhat quieter and more relaxed but sustainable pace.

I happened to be based in London during the times of Thatcherism. The United Kingdom was attuning itself to the spirit of buy-British, the scuttling of unprofitable industries and the discovery on a significant scale of new talent, new businesses and new lines of work. It lies in human nature to rise to meet challenges rather than lying down, accepting defeat, as long as all that happens on a scale that does not crush the country but is survivable. So the Brits will be OK.

What is going to happen to the American economy? Internationally, looking at it from their point of view, a safe bet will be: not an awful lot. People will reassess their priorities, cut back on spending and use their purchasing power wisely. Internally, within the framework of the American economy, there will be dramatic change. After suffering through initial losses with a lot of individual hardship and a lowering of living standards many people will come to discover that the situation offers new opportunities to many.

Buy-British under Thatcher will pale into insignificance compared to what we shall witness once the Americans have regained their undiminished self-confidence, roll up their sleeves or – more likely in our times – buy new T-shirts, displaying the appropriate mottos. I can think of a few and I am certainly by no means the only one. 'Buy-American' would be at the most conservative end of things, with a number of uplifting ones like 'let's show 'em!', 'the sky's the limit!' and of course 'we can do it!' It has always been a mistake to write off the Americans and it would be an unwise choice now.

Let us face it: in a country the size of the United States the sky really *is* the limit. If you have ever been on a hiking trip in Death Valley, thinking of the early settlers that made it through there in their covered wagons and succeeded or the way in which the country took on and met simultaneously and in parallel the threat of Imperial Japan and Nazi Germany and succeeded, it would be naïve to think that America will go to its knees in a weakened world economy. They will do whatever it takes and then come out stronger. Who said it would be easy, but they can and will come out on top.

So where does all that leave the world champion of exports, with no significant domestic market, a sophisticated, expensive to run state, huge statutory budgetary demands and no Mediterranean sun shining on it to give people something to brighten up their days? The 1970s marked the end of the boom years. Since then the country has been gradually building up a huge national debt. There is not a living soul in Germany that can even remotely show you a realistic and reliable plan how that is going to be worked off.

Ever!

When I first wrote the following section GDP in 2008/9 had fallen by five to six per cent and industrial production in some industries by as much as 17.5 to 25 per cent, subject to what statistics you use. Unemployment figures showed something like seven to ten per cent of the population out of work and having been so for a long time, depending on how you rated *Kurzarbeit*, the so called short-work, people not really in full-time employment but hanging on to their jobs with part subsidies by the government and numerous people being re-trained at modest income and thus taken out of the unemployment statistics.

Since then Germany has come out of that recession, seemingly stronger than before. But that is deceptive. Much of the resurgence in employment was made possible by dramatic changes in social-security legislation, first introduced under Chancellor Gerhard Schroeder as his Agenda 2010, which resulted in widespread cutting-back on unemployment and other benefits. As a result many have now dropped below the poverty-line, struggling through on subsistence income, many needing more than one job to make ends meet. Appearances may be friendly, seen from the angle of national economy, masking new misery at the lower end of the scale and adding to a stratum of lingering unease.

We know that there exists admirable solidarity in the country, keeping things ticking and people in bread. But the social legislation surrounding the Agenda 2010 has shifted the burden from business and industry to the individual common man or woman. The social market economy was given a kick in the back and replaced by opportunism of the few in positions of power against the many in positions of need and without power.

This has laid the foundation for smouldering, slowly growing discontent.

For a number of years the government has been signalling better times ahead, suggesting that any setbacks are temporary, surely more than overcome once the economy picks up again and things get back to normal. The economy did pick up again but things did *not* get back to normal for too many people. Those in positions of power and influence seem to be insensitive, having given in to a climate of greed.

Currently the mainstay of German exporting industry includes luxury cars, high-class apparel and sophisticated industrial plant and equipment. The latter market segment may be short-lived. It serves to boost industries in countries that will become the competitors of tomorrow of the Germans with a fast emerging industrial base of their own.

But what if the decline of 2008/9 *is* normal, the level of activities *being* the appropriate scale of things? From where do the country's decision makers get the notion that despite diminishing demand in their traditional buyer-countries, new competitors from Asia, a looming energy crisis and impending climate change things *will* pick up dramatically?

Are the Germans masters at denial, turning a blind eye on unpleasant things, willing them to go away? Listening to some of the pep-talk coming out of Berlin these days one might be forgiven for thinking that they are whistling in the dark, groping for clues and not really knowing where the country is going.

There is another explanation for why things are the way they are. The country's political and electoral system is making it impossible to establish clear-cut parliamentary majorities on which effective government can be based that will see the country through the many challenges of today. To have any government at all there has to be a parliamentary coalition between extant political parties that will secure majorities so that whatever they want to achieve can be carried by majority vote.

Traditionally the Federal Republic had two large parties, called Volksparteien, the CDU Christian Democrat Conservatives, with an autonomous wing in Bavaria, the CSU Christian-Social Union, and the SPD Socialists. Their respective shares of the popular vote were such, that in a coalition with the lesser third force, the Liberals, one of the Volksparteien could establish parliamentary majority or on occasion go it alone.

Ultra-right-wing groups or communists never became a decisive element. Things changed with the advent of The Greens, which became so significant that they could form a coalition government under Chancellor Gerhard Schroeder. German unification added yet another parliamentary faction which after merging with defectors from the Socialists has established itself as *Die Linke*, the Left, so that there are now five parties regularly collecting in excess of five per cent of the popular vote, counting the CDU/CSU as one. A sixth party has emerged, so far at state level, the *Piratenpartei*, the Pirates; it remains to be seen whether they make the five per cent hurdle in federal elections or whether they were only a brief signal of voter discontent. As per the latest national parliamentary elections for the Bundestag the Liberals slipped below the five-percent hurdle and are no longer represented in the federal parliament, thereby depriving the CDU/CSU of their favourite coalition partner. The consequences of that have yet to manifest themselves.

Whilst seemingly giving voters a wider choice this has made the forming of coalitions that will command a majority in parliament more difficult. During election campaigns the parties will present their programs or platforms. When government coalitions emerge, these will be based on an agreement between the parties forming the coalition, called *Koalitionsvertrag*, which is meant to give them a majority in parliament. The Koalitionsvertrag is usually based on extensive haggling and compromising and is supposed to form the basis for the conduct of government business during the forthcoming legislative period, usually four years. That is the regular interval between scheduled parliamentary elections for the Bundestag.

Under this process the respective party leaders will enjoy limited freedom as to how to exercise their powers. Whatever they wish to accomplish has to be reconcilable with the Koalitionsvertrag. It does not require much imagination to see to what extent the voter has a say in running things. He has delegated his sovereign authority, granted by the country's constitution, to a political party, which has two choices: stick it out on strict adherence to how they see the will of the voter or make the best of it, enter into compromises acceptable to coalition parties so that they can then share power and set up government.

If you were to apply this management model to running a business, chances are that this would not work for very long and that the business in question would hardly prosper or succeed.

If this were all there is it would be too easy and too good to be true. Germany is a Federal Republic with sixteen States, called *Bundesland*. Each of them has a state parliament elected by general vote, very much along the same lines as the federal parliament, with the same choice of political parties but not necessarily the same parliamentary majorities as outcome. Same as at national level there are governments for each one of the states with a prime minister at its head, called first or governing mayor in the so called *Stadtstaaten* or city states of Berlin, Bremen and Hamburg. Representatives from the states will make up the *Bundesrat*, the assembly of the representatives of the states. A number of legislative processes require endorsement by the Bundesrat, in particular anything that will in any way change the set-up of the Bundesrepublik.

At present all states have coalition governments, constituted through a similar process as that which produces the Federal Government. These will reflect parliamentary majorities at state level, some showing the lead party constituting the Bundestag at the helm, some dominated by the party that is in the opposition role at federal level. Thus Bundesrat decisions are not necessarily a foregone conclusion and may not reflect the power structure at federal level. There have been times when both the leading and the major opposition party at federal level controlled an equal number of states, leading to what the Germans call a Pat-Situation, a parliamentary deadlock, with no majority decision possible. That comes pretty close to a Mexican stand-off without the risk of shooting, of which the long and the short is that nothing decisive will come from it.

So these are the management tools that Germany has at its disposal to steer the country through the challenges constituted by our modern, globalised world. It does not require a lot of imagination to see that this dos not exactly favour quick response, nor will it enhance the pioneering of bold, far-reaching decisions. Whilst they are all entitled to having their good intentions, the political parties that effectively constitute the power-base that runs the country and sets the course for the future are limited in their influence to that which they can get agreed and secured in coalitions at federal and state level. Each new federal or state government will be limited to a maximum term of office of four years, five in some states, until the next election will most likely lead to a different coalition, a different placing of accents on priorities and a different main thrust to reflect whatever any new coalition wants to see accomplished.

How hard will it be to agree with Germany's much revered poet Heinrich Heine, who during the middle of the Nineteenth Century had to leave the country for political reasons, when you weigh all this in your mind to assess the potential effectiveness of Germany's political system?

> Heine said: *denk ich an Deutschland bei der Nacht, werd' ich um meinen Schlaf gebracht, which translates into Germany gives me many a sleepless night, not quite literally.*

After Heine's sleepless nights Germany had to endure the creation of the Empire, World Wars I and II, Hitler and the Holocaust. Who wants to deny that he must have had visions that gave him a sense of utmost unease? The Germans have created an impressive number of remarkable things. Do they have the right tools at their disposal to keep the ship in safe channels?

Ora et Labora - Pray and Work

The German economy is all about gainful employment and wealth creation. In order to understand the country's economic scene we need to take a closer look at what is commonly referred to as *work*, sometimes *labour* and the rewards it may generate and sometimes it is discussed along these lines:

Since the Creation man has enjoyed the God-given right to work.

That is of course nonsense. Work was not the result of divine creation but the necessity for humans to secure their livelihood, which among other things encompasses eating, drinking, the pursuit of happiness and a few other items. All this requires money, be it earned or inherited and we have already ruled out stolen. In earlier times there was that mysteriously untraceable 'voice-from-above' with friendly advice like 'he who shall not work shall not eat', of which there exist various versions. But they all have more or less in common that it pleases our maker if we work for our living.

In Germany round about the early nineteenth century 'ora et labora', pray and work, became the mantra of 'Hanseatic' merchants, meaning from Hamburg and other affluent trading centres and 'Calvinist' factory owners, meaning the predominantly protestant upper crust, the crème of emerging German wealth. It fuelled a general feeling of 'work is great' and helped to press maximum commitment and efficiency out of the workforce. There was an undertone that God would love you more that way and steer earthly rewards in your direction, whilst you should not forget to drop a fair portion of it in the lap of the Church.

This pretty well pins down the moment in history at which work as we know it today was invented. It really makes no difference, whether we consider it to herald the emerging industrial age or whether this philosophy became one of the cornerstones of our modern economy. Rapidly advancing industrialisation triggered off equally rapid growth of hitherto unknown wealth in the hands of *few*, whilst the *many* were more or less happy to work to exhaustion - at least for a while.

Industrial manufacturing of goods reversed the underlying fundamental principles. 'Working to achieve an objective' or, less pompously, 'working to get done something that was needed', was replaced by 'working to make money', which more often than not was embellished by allusions to the divine blessing that accompanied the process. In the end one part of the population thereby became very rich and another derived satisfaction from being good at helping them with it. If I had to pull names out of the hat to illustrate the process I would nominate James Watt with his invention of the steam engine and Messrs. Malthus and Smith who came up with a plausible philosophy to confirm this. Their inventions and teachings were the forerunners of globalisation. Work was no longer the means to an end. It had become an end in itself.

Work from this moment onwards served only one purpose: to make money, make it on the back of more money and make it by breaking the back of the people who earn it for us. With that we have arrived at the threshold of our modern world, which is structured around the principle of self-centred industry for maximum gain. The availability of machines made it possible to manufacture more goods than were needed for one's own use, which led to their mass production. You can read this concurrently with the advent of the industrial age or the rise of German industry in the Nineteenth Century. It hardly makes a difference.

Once you start going down that route you cross the point at which you enter into the death-spiral of making more goods, to make more money, to expand your industrial capabilities, to make more goods to amortise the money invested in your machines that will help you to make more money . . . and an uncontrollable element of greed creeps into the setup.

When we have saturated our own home market we go abroad . . . farther and farther afield until we come to the limits of our naturally grown economy. Instead of consolidating what we have achieved we continue to expand, 'importing' labour as we have outstripped our own capacities. As we continue to expand we discover the blessings of farming out parts of the manufacturing process to smaller companies that can work more cheaply, some at home, some abroad. We do this to become more competitive and open up an even greater market.

As we do that we need fewer workers. Business flourishes whilst unemployment creeps in and starts rising. As we farm out sub-contracts, smaller, high-yield domestic companies are squeezed out of business and our industrial base re-structures itself: high-value gains now accrue to the subcontractors abroad while we manage happily with a combination of the smallest number possible of highly paid high performers, supported by minimum-wage helpers, the fewer the better.

Looking back we find that we have scuttled medium to small sized businesses, got rid of subsistence to small farming and are happily importing produce that we could just as well grow at home. Employment statistics for the numbers involved in the process stayed more or less the same – we just traded off our expensive domestic labour base for an over all cheaper one, made up of elements at home and abroad, 'optimised'.

In Germany on the back of this we now have some ten out of about eighty-two million people out of work or indirectly affected as family members of the unemployed. Some twelve million or fifteen per cent of the population have slipped below the poverty line, many struggling on starvation income, some needing three jobs to make ends meet. At the same time we look for more trained people from abroad as our sixteen independent state school systems don't talk to each other and cannot sufficiently train and educate some one to two million young people living right now in our midst, written off and left by the wayside. Industry considers them to be unfit or unsuitable to meet their standards and they are relegated to aid and welfare programs. And yet, Germany continues to rank among the top three to four industrial and exporting nations in the world.

Wow!

That in a much over-simplified way characterises the point at which a significant part of Germany's big industry finds itself today, wrapped up in these highlights:

- Big manufacturing industry (short BMI) has 'optimised' itself, playing off a maximum of highly efficient capital based production assets vs. the strictest minimum of absolutely necessary workers

- BMI is global in the truest sense of the word, minimising cost through international production sharing in conjunction with often elaborate schemes to reduce or completely avoid taxation in Germany

- For Germany at the end of this process looms the spectre of having next to no highly qualified and high-yield domestic workforce and almost no tax income from BMI whilst German industry generates its profits abroad with the help of secure tax-havens, from where they filter back along inconspicuous if not outright mysterious channels into the hands of the business owners, more or less tax-free

If the above is true, what other factors are there, that keep the German economy not merely going but doing great? That looks like a bit of a mystery. Let us go back to the beginning, i.e. the early days of Germany as a nation state, to try and get an insight into how the young German state was wired, how the foundation was laid to structures that have lasted to this day. The proclamation of the German Empire triggered off an atmosphere of pride and ambition that can be wrapped up in these words:

Now we are somebody . . . let's go show them.

In the second half of the nineteenth century Great Britain, then still widely referred to as England, was the leading industrial and military power in Europe. From day one Germany was obsessed to become just that. All over Europe nationalism was up in the air.

A rush to claim colonies in remote parts of the world set in that hitherto had been overlooked in Phase 1by the front-runners Portugal and Spain. They had colonised South America. England and France divided up vast parts of Africa between them, India and Indo-China. Being late arrivals on the scene the Germans had to settle for several colonies in Africa, parts of New Guinea, a few islands in the Pacific and the city and surroundings of Tsingtao in China, in all an assortment of leftovers. All the more the Germans pounced on them with a vengeance.

The only convenient way to reach these colonies from Germany was by sea. This led to a vigorous campaign to build warships for the Imperial German Navy and create an impressive merchant fleet. In parallel with shipbuilding the strengthening of military land forces received priority status. After all, one needed an efficient and effective army; just in case. At the same time railways were built at a staggering pace. It was rumoured that revenues from the German railways widely served to finance the new imperial navy. Industrialisation and with it electrification advanced swiftly.

All this served to provide a solid customer base for Germany's rapidly developing mining, heavy, electrical and chemical industries. Many of these started as family businesses and grew into industrial giants with names like Thyssen, Krupp, Borsig, Siemens and Henschel, fast gaining world-wide recognition.

The concept of the family business was very much in line with the sociological fabric and fibre of authoritarian traditions with one principal at the top and undisputed loyalty down to the last apprentice and back up again. The workforce stood by their superiors with total dedication and trust. Often a sense of pride and admiration took hold. Employees of Krupp, the industrial giant that grew famous for building canons and railways, proudly referred to themselves as 'kruppianers', totally identifying with the enterprise. This is merely one example that can stand for many to illustrate the spirit that had taken possession of Germany at the end of the nineteenth century: not only *were* we somebody – we were *going* somewhere!

In keeping with ancient traditions of especially Prussian aristocracy those at the head of a company assumed obligations that went way beyond paying wages for the work carried out, building vast housing estates to accommodate their workforce with schools, medical facilities and in some cases even churches. That very much helped to keep out labour disputes.

Despite continuing to remain an absolute monarchy the country received a parliament with its seat at the Reichstag Building, the national assembly in Berlin, which derived its authority as much from the grace of God as consent by the emperor. A good way to describe the prevailing form of government may be benevolent tyranny. It had been a clever move for which Chancellor Bismarck can take credit, which served to steer potential unrest into orderly and easily controllable channels, a truly Prussian approach. One of these measures was the so called *Sozialgesetzgebung*, general and comprehensive social legislation. Although it was handed down to the workers, i.e. given to them instead of having been fought for and earned, it was of such quality that it greatly obviated the need for any protracted struggle for workers' rights, giving them a framework of conditions that defined their position and would stand up in court., if need be. Some of the fundamental principles of that early legislation can still be found in German labour law of today.

All this served to enhance productivity, increase industrial output and make Germany into an affluent country with competent industries at the height of the state of the art, good industrial management and a dedicated workforce.

And in World War I they gambled all of it away in a huge and dramatic shot to nothing that due to false pride and the inability to communicate erupted over trivia, plunged parts of the world into chaos and misery and served to destroy much of the economic base that the Germans had created for themselves.

At this point something more tangible than a one-minute silence would be appropriate to underline consternation and sadness over the lack of rationality that had misguided Germany; a modern, civilised, leading industrial nation that had thrown away what it had worked so hard to acquire ever since its first breath. Well, not all was thrown away and lost. In the country there now remained a defiant spirit of past greatness. People had something to aspire to again, come the right moment.

Germany more struggled through than bounced back after the war and into a tumultuous phase of government in the Weimar Republic. Economically it meant stagnation at best and no significant advancement on any front. But despite heavy-handed interference by the victors, in particular France and England, Germany's industrial base remained widely intact, ready to take off again.

The take-off came under Hitler and his totalitarian Third Reich, which pounced on the extant industrial base to turn it into a callously conceived war industry that served only one purpose: to reach out for domination of Germany, its neighbouring countries and as much of the world as possible. Helped by the prevalence of traditional authoritarian structures the benevolent tyranny gave way to one from which the word benevolent had been removed while strengthening the tyranny aspect.

The rest is history: the world was thrown into chaos once again, and after that, miraculously, Germany yet again was granted another lease of life. Once rebuilding the country got under way after World War II the combined effects of finance from Marshall Plan and *Lastenausgleich*, Burden Sharing, a limitless market and the availability of an industrious, competent workforce with energetic management served to create what soon came to be known as the German *Wirtschaftswunder*, the Economic Miracle. Total destruction of many industrial facilities came to serve as a blessing in disguise. The necessity to replace them effectively re-equipped Germany, the losers of the war, with new equipment whilst the winner countries had to struggle on with obsolescent machinery that had come

92

through the war intact, thereby putting them at a significant disadvantage.

All went well for Germany until 1971, the year that marks a dramatic change in trends: the workforce wanted more money, prices of German products went up and competitiveness down, the national economic growth curve flattened and the country for the first time in its young history went into deficit spending, national expenditure outperforming national income.

Since that time the country has not come back from overspending, save for tiny hints from time to time, hardly noticeable and not sustainable. And this is the second economic miracle: how can Germany retain its position as the leading European economic power and one of the top four in the world, despite apparent deficiencies in the educational system and farming out abroad significant parts of its manufacturing and prime income generating base?

After some soul searching and a prolonged thinking process, not claiming to have become privy to the ultimate truth, I have come up with a three parts answer. I do not particularly like any one of these parts and they appear to be reasonably plausible:

- Germany has been subsidising its industrial output to the tune of an accrued deficit of well over €2,000,000,000,000 thereby effectively buying a market-share, funded by an ever increasing deficit, of which nobody really knows how it is going to be repaid, if ever.

- My criticism of remnants of an authoritarian state may have masked the fact that these could be strength rather than weakness, up to a point, enhancing Germany's chances of success. If you think of China, Japan and Germany, on the one hand, all with varying degrees of authoritarian elements in their industrial culture and the United States, a democracy on the other, you get a 3:1 ratio in favour of economies of an authoritarian persuasion. Such a rather crude and un-scientific statement may cause raised eyebrows in other countries but inasmuch as Germany is concerned I know what I am talking about. The German language renders itself to creating what I call 'word-monsters', one such monster being *'vorauseilender Gehorsam'*, meaning to obey and carry out orders before they are given. This is of course far from anything resembling a science-based approach, just a feeling and very much open to educated debate. But it is there, for us to think about. In the absence of clearly defined and readily available individual personal rights it was prudent to please those above you - and the phenomenon has not become extinct. Off the record and with no ladies present one might hear such allusions as 'crawling up the colon of somebody, rather than giving them the straight and level right to their face'. Put differently and already stated: opportunism flourished.

- My third point is the suspicion that our economic world is undergoing significant change: private sector economic power houses now shape the international economic scene, pushing national economies into the background. That could explain why national governments increasingly appear helpless, chasing international economic events rather than shaping them. That is quite frightening if one thinks it through to its possible ultimate conclusion.

The question is: who has the say in Germany and shapes its decision making processes? I offer you multiple choices:

- The citizen and voter
- The political parties
- The elected members of the German parliament
- The federal government or
- An unknown and as yet unidentified power behind any one of these, behind the scenes or totally disconnected from anything else

What if it were the latter one? Or is it anyone or anything else outside the above, keeping a low profile? Having been in charge over some forty years - on and off - of analysing and understanding situations and forecasting which way things are likely to go I developed a certain sensitivity. It says that at this point in time in Germany the 'good ones' are really good and totally dependable. But there may be some 'baddies' in the wings whose prime concern is not the welfare of the nation, let alone humankind in the widest sense.

And that is where the danger lurks.

We have unshaken trust in the dedicated few, but what about the others, those that do not have the country's welfare as their prime concern and are lured and steered on their way by some other, undisclosed and potentially sinister cause?

Sustainability and the Myth of Unlimited Growth

The magic word for everything we do is sustainability. In nature only that which continues to reproduce in an unforced way is sustainable and survives, that which does not perishes. Allusions to the survival of the fittest relate to the fact that nature is uncompromising. That should serve as guidance for how we shape our little world. If we lose sight of this fundamental principle, we lose that which we create.

This applies to our immediate surroundings as well as the country, its economy and GDP and the role it plays in the world. German history is a stark reminder. Its activities leading up to the Empire, the Third Reich and the two World Wars were unsustainable and resulted both times in the collapse of the country.

One of the things that motivate me to write this book is to fathom out whether the root causes of World Wars I and II have been dealt with definitively. There exists general consensus that unresolved issues from World War I favoured the Nazis' rise to power, with World War II as their dreadful consequence. After 1918 such unresolved issues primarily included hurt pride and resentment over losing the war and its shameful outcome as seen from the German side. But even more so there had been the Germans' quest for becoming and continuing to be a leading world power, which had been thwarted by the outcome of the war. Hitler may have seen this as an open wound that could be used to stir up and manipulate emotions to channel the country's energies to that aim.

The Germans not only lost both conflicts, at the end of World War II they also lost vast parts of the country as reparations for launching unprovoked wars of aggression on Poland and the Soviet Union. Yet both times the Germans came back in a definitive way, after 1945 throwing all their energies into becoming a leading economic power, at which they have obviously succeeded.

Yet many people both in Germany and abroad have a sense of unease. One senses that there exists an emotional mortgage from a shady past that continues to lurk below the surface, close enough to break through again as and when certain factors come together. One does not really gain the conviction that whatever happened in the past is over and done with, deserving to be put to rest once and for all. Is there perhaps something in the mindset of the country, a latent preparedness to do the unexpected? Germany's strength is no longer military; Germany has become the leading economic power in Europe. Therefore, if economic strength is the determining factor, that would be the key to understanding and assessing the situation.

There exists no such thing as unlimited growth. Every development in nature as well as in business life will strive towards its characteristic maximum or endpoint, stagnate when this is reached and may shrink, decline or collapse having gone past it. Throughout history new replaced old and long familiar scenarios became obsolete. We should be open for innovation and not cling at all cost to things to which we have become accustomed, seeking to perpetuate them and resisting change. Who knows, something better may replace those things that we give up.

Practically all industrial societies have become dependent on what is commonly referred to as 'growth', best exemplified by general domestic product or GDP - that grows . . . and grows . . . and grows - seemingly with no end. They need growth for one very simple reason: they have been unable to contain national expenditure within the limits of available and thereby disposable national resources and income. In addition to national expenditure, which is needed to fuel the country's economy and generate income, there is another element: let us call it 'friction', which encompasses all the things that a country does not really need and which do not contribute to its economic well-being. They may be due to the lack of budgetary discipline, a country's 'affluent lifestyle', doing or buying things it cannot really afford or political concessions to please the voter and thereby keep the governing party in power.

When economies got going again after disruption by World War II there existed a seemingly unlimited market to rebuild and resupply to make up for war damages and losses, made possible through readily available funding from the American Marshall Plan and in the case of Germany the *Lastenausgleich*, Burden Sharing. Markets grew and expanded naturally due to increased demand, met by an increased ability to manufacture and supply. Growth became a fact of life: national budgets grew as did income. But in order to function smoothly this scenario needed the continued existence of a readily available market to absorb output that expanded or grew continuously; phrased differently: an unlimited market.

Of course Germany was not the only country with an expanding industrial capacity, meeting the required quality standards at competitive product pricing. More and more countries and their manufacturers entered the market at an ever increasing rate, competing with Germany.

At the same time efficiency and quality standards in the countries commonly referred to as 'emerging markets' increased steadily along with their degree of self-sufficiency. This reduced their need for outside suppliers and put traditional suppliers increasingly under pressure, among them Germany. As a consequence growth potential for traditional supplier countries like Germany has steadily diminished or disappeared completely for some product categories and markets, more and more relegating Germany's industry to a niche of sophisticated, high-value products, where the competition does not yet meet standards. The instrument of unlimited growth is no longer readily available. It is even on the decline in essential core market segments.

This is the classical dilemma of practically all highly developed countries that depend on growing national income to keep in step with growing expenditure, whilst in fact the economy may be shrinking. There exist no such things as unlimited markets, growth or income. Everything in nature as well as in life at some point reaches its limits – a well-known fact since time immemorial. It is just not always convenient to face up to it. So the situation arrives where there would have been the appropriate moment to engage in creative thinking, to prepare for suitable policy changes. Alas, more often than not nothing of the sort is done.

It may be possible to mask the effects of shrinking or disappearing market segments for some time, but sooner or later there comes the moment of truth, at which one has to face the consequences. At that stage a country broadly speaking has three options:

- Make sure that you put all your activities on a healthy footing and manage within the limitations imposed by readily available income

- Subsidise your economy through debt finance, borrowing money from creditors to close the gap and carry on as before

- If nobody will lend you money and the gap cannot be closed- go into bankruptcy

There are a number of countries that go on happily in category No 1 and manage within the scope of their readily available means. The current debt crisis is about a number of countries which for whatever reason are unable to do that and need outside funding to balance the books.

Among them are some seemingly shaky ones. Amazingly they are showered with a mixture of mild reproach to unspoken contempt by Germany, whose total accumulated debt is more than that of many of the other countries combined. Germany's financiers do not seem to have a problem with that as long as they can pass the buck. It is a bit like playing at musical chairs, where you have to make sure to have a chair to sit on when the music stops. But if Germany underwrites everybody else's debt on top of having its own to contend with that places Germany at the very top of the mountain of debt. What will happen if the music actually does stop, doing so at an unexpected and inconvenient moment?

The result could be an upheaval as severe as the closing stages of World War II.

What has to happen so that it does not come to that?

There is one solid truth: economies whose principals are unable or unwilling to reconcile their outlook and actions with known facts of life are bound to fail unless they can manage a decisive turn-around before the last call has come and gone.

Germany as one of the leading industrial countries needs a totally new perspective and fresh outlook.

In many ways the development of Germany's economy has gone down the same route as that of most other industrial countries, which all have in common that they are more or less heavily dependent on steady growth. A balanced economy is one where the aggregate total of expenditure stays comfortably below that of income or, in other words, revenues received covers both production costs and all administrative and other overheads, put into the language of commerce and industry.

In the case of Germany and a number of other countries that is not the case. The country does not generate enough income and therefore has to subsidise its economy. To pay for that there are broadly speaking three legitimate options and a criminal one:

1. Ask the taxpayer for more money

2. Sell the family silver

3. Borrow

4. Steal other countries' treasures as widely done in the not so distant past by the Nazis

Germany does not appear to apply options 1 and 2 of the above. German taxation levels are not excessive and the country does not really have a lot of tangible assets that it could sell, even if it wanted to, which primarily leaves option 3, which is currently widely exercised.

Is there perhaps more?

We can certainly rule out option 4, can't we? Nobody would have such bad taste and ill manners to openly accuse a trusted friend and ally of stealing. But perhaps there *does* exist a grey area where something is neither outright good nor outright bad, where the word 'murky' comes to mind. Since time immemorial it has been frowned upon if a merchant knowingly sells goods to someone that cannot really afford or does not need them and to compound the irony of the situation rather 'generously' extends to the buyer all necessary credit facilities so that the transaction can go through. In such a case one often speaks of *hard* or *over-selling*.

Such a case of hard selling may have occurred when the Germans sold submarines to the Greeks and financed them. The only conceivable enemy against whom the Greeks could use submarines would be the Turks, a trusted friend and ally in NATO, same as the Greeks. Against all other potential enemies Greece would be sheltered under the umbrella of NATO.

We can assume that NATO would not stand idly by to permit a war between Greece and Turkey, two of their members. If one were to dig deep enough this may very well turn out to be a cleverly disguised case of egomania, where the Greek admirals said if the Turks have submarines so must we and the Germans 'unselfishly' stepped in as willing helpers, regardless of any necessity; or did they simply step in to get more work for their shipyards, never mind necessity or morality?

When the international financial situation in Europe started running out of control Greece was one of the first countries in the line of fire for overspending and excessive borrowing. It wasn't just submarines. Primarily German makers of high-value luxury items happily sold to the Greeks whatever they wanted and financed it irrespective of need and affordability. And finance was not always cheap nor was it always competitive, if you apply fair market conditions, say by putting the finance out to competing third parties.

The Germans could have alleviated the burden on the Greek economy by honouring claims for war damages that go back to World War II, pay up once and for all and close a big gap in the Greek national budget. Alas they have so far not done that.

Greece is one of many countries that ran into the trap of hard-selling luxury items along with 'convenient' finance. In normal business and in most countries that which we call 'loan sharking' is frowned upon if not a crime, extending credit at exaggerated rates. The Germans would not strictly have done that but the mere fact of making finance available that is neither needed nor affordable at, shall we say, 'slightly' above market rates, causes suspicion. This suspicion is aggravated by the fact that the Germans have been subsidising their exporting industries through creating favourable tax conditions for their manufacturers and exporters. Being themselves lenders on a grand scale they were able to borrow more cheaply than their customers, whose business boosted their credit rating. Another allegory from murky business practices comes to mind: chain letters, illegal in most countries. What the Germans have been doing was still not quite that and would not have been punishable by law. It would just have been grossly unfair and devoid of the prudence and foresight of the good merchant, who will have the long-term welfare of his customers at heart. One word comes to mind when we look at the situation: this suggests an ambition towards *market domination*, which in political terms translates into *the quest for economic hegemony*.

Someone of importance - I forget who - once said that war is the continuation of diplomacy by military means. Many wars are fought if someone very much wants to be number one. In that case we speak of wars for hegemony. Leading German car makers have openly declared their goal at either becoming or being the number one car maker in the world. Is that a quest for economic hegemony? Being successful in business is one thing but boosting it with a vengeance whilst subsidising it so as to beat the competition is not good business practice.

It may be a question of scale: if it is small enough it may be annoying to the competition; if the dimension deserves the adjective 'global' that then is a quest for hegemony. In the past the amazing thing about the Germans was that more than once they were able to get so far ahead although they had no money. But they had something even more important: they had an excellent credit rating or economic clout. Hitler's credit rating was good until the debacle at Stalingrad and then it went through the floor. But credit rating or not: in World War II the Germans knew and planned from the outset that in the end they would *definitely not* pay up.

That was no more and no less than economic scorched earth policy.

I really resent having to go back to past history every so often when looking at the Germany of today. Yet it is somehow unavoidable. If you want to assess development potential and the inherent risks you are obliged to take into consideration past performance same as any banker will do before mortgaging your annex to the garden shed. This is just a question of scale: the same criteria apply irrespective of size and volume.

Today not many would be likely to agree with me if I were to say the Germans are at an advanced stage of the quest for economic hegemony in Europe. If I went one step further to speak of economic conflict short of an outright economic war there would be violent protest.

Deservedly so?

Let me put this into perspective: I do not think that the Germans would knowingly and with intent do something so dramatic as to knock international economy out of balance, but they might do so inadvertently, being unaware of the consequences of some of their actions, in particular their 'success'. Have you heard of the King Midas Syndrome, whereby an over-abundance of material wealth becomes totally useless?

We are in a grey if not murky area of defining things with adequate clarity. There are the many little tell-tale signs that I find so hard to reconcile with my definition of the fair and just conduct of business.

Germany has many strong and powerful industries that have set the world standard, the most glamorous one being the motor industry. Large German carmakers have been buying if not to say snapping up car manufacturers in several countries. A spectacular case was Seat of Spain, subsequently followed by Skoda of Czechoslovakia, which became the Czech and Slovak Republics. Political narrative at the time described the acquisitions as 'good Samaritan ship'.

If we really think of Europe as a family of nations, would it not have been fairer to help these two companies get back on their feet through partnership arrangements? I agree that such a notion is not supported by modern industry in the widest sense, which epitomises competition and quest for domination. But to me that is just so much more scorched earth. When you buy up large companies in other countries it is like colonising a part of the local population.

That is Nineteenth Century – not today's world.

Perhaps this will continue to work until some greater event signals the need for change. Stalingrad in World War II was the long-needed eye-opener for those that had not wanted to see. The near collapse of a number of economies in Europe and elsewhere should be the eye-opener that we need today. Could it be that we are already right in the middle of some kind of Economic World War III?

It is high time for a dramatic and comprehensive re-appraisal of our economic and political world, whilst an ever-increasing occurrence of natural disasters serves as a reminder that the socio-economic cosmos that we have been so fondly used to has come to its natural limits.

Something desperately needs to change . . . or else . . . .

The Demise of Germany's Middle Class

Traditionally modern countries have had an upper class, those that own and run things, a lower class, those that do the work and between the two the middle class for everything else, give or take a little. The backbone of this latter one has been small business and trade and the arts and crafts. Since the formation of the Federal Republic this latter segment has undergone dramatic change. A contiguous network of small, often specialised shops and stores has had to give way to a far smaller number of strategically placed markets, often called 'super-market', serving a large catchment area with a comprehensive choice of articles from food to household goods, often including children's wear and even bicycles, sporting goods, car parts and accessories. Whilst shops and stores had been located bordering on residential areas or even right in their middle, many of the modern markets are located on 'green-fields-sites' in the truest sense, often located with an eye to offering good access by road, i. e. by car and mostly out of reach for access on foot.

Whilst shops and stores had mostly been family businesses that drew their staff from the neighbourhood the markets recruited their personnel under aspects of minimising cost with no sociological connotation, i. e. regardless of where they lived, as long as they accepted the pay and took care of how they commuted to the workplace. This shift deprived many shop and store owners and their families of their source of income and their social status. It had particularly grave effects on their children that thereby lost their social identity and a sense of belonging. The markets also brought about a dramatic change in the sourcing, supplying and distributing of food stuffs, mostly cutting out local or even regional farming in favour of large-scale supplies bought from far afield, selected in accordance with availability and cost criteria. That practically meant the end to local subsistence and small-scale farming. On top of that EEC and later EU-European regulations did the rest, favouring larger businesses and ultimately helping to pull the rug from under the feet of the small farmers. Those that could retired, others used up their savings or other income, became workers or simply unemployed. This is, of course, a phenomenon that has affected all modern countries, some more so, some less, but the change in the sociological makeup of society has been significant and visible to the naked eye in the appearance of residential areas and suburbs, deprived of their local small businesses.

Due to their far greater bargaining power the markets were able to significantly lower price levels in a number of fields. As they purchased on a global scale certain seasonal produce became available irrespective of the time of year, which put local, seasonal produce at a disadvantage, as the purchasers acting for the markets wanted a uniform, year-round supply, which they could assure by optimising seasonal availability on a global scale.

This scenario brought out the price-sensitive bargain-hunters, which favoured volume supplies at steady pricing over best possible quality for the season and not necessarily the cheapest, thereby compounding the negative trend that was running against the middle class merchants and suppliers. As a consequence, even the top-corner stores were unable to compete. Product diversity was sacrificed to 'what's cheapest and always there'.

Produce bought in large quantities and from far away needs transportation, which means an additional burden on the country's transport infrastructure. This in turn leads to a heavier burden on imported fuels, wear and tear on roads and bridges and more air pollution from fuel-burn and rubber wear-off from car and truck tires. These latter aspects find their way into public budgets for road and bridge maintenance, repair and eventual renewal, which are only partly covered by road-tax and motorway tolls.

One very significant aspect is the large-scale export of jobs. Local shop and store personnel and the farming community lost jobs that are now serving the economies in countries abroad. Far from wanting to take a rather chauvinist view I want to emphasise that we should seek to balance economic conditions in our own surroundings before reaching out abroad. I do believe in international cooperation where this makes sense.

In the case of Germany I would not lay the blame on the markets and their suppliers. It has been the German government, first and foremost, that failed to see and understand the problems facing the middle class, pampering instead large businesses and industries that, mistakenly as I think, are seen as comprising large blocks of voters. And there is one other, potentially highly precarious aspect that has been created by the government's failure to safeguard the country's middle class.

When everything collapsed at the end of World War II the middle class proved to be best endowed to master the challenge on account of what they *knew* how to do and were *able* to do: *survive*.

What if we ever need that again?

Due to the failures and errors of those politically responsible, which would have been in a position to make a difference, the aspect of care for the common good has vanished completely from this segment of the economy. It is high time to remind ourselves that we shall fare best when the common good flourishes, not when a relatively small number of people accumulate great riches.

A Country without Elite?

Rebuilding Germany met with two serious problems:

1. Those potentially available for leadership positions had no historic background to draw on of what a desirable state-culture should be. There existed no traditional elements that could safely be blended into the fabric and fibre of the new democratic state. For the younger ones Nazi-Germany was all they knew, those able to go back in memory focused on the so called 'good-old-times' of imperial Germany with the infallible authority of the emperor. Other examples from own experience were practically not available. The period of some fifteen years of the Weimar Republic between the wars was widely dismissed as chaotic, not setting an example to be followed.

2. The new leadership had to be picked from what Nazi rule and war had left over. The persecution of the Jewish population, dissidents and members of various minorities had eliminated a large segment of the population that would normally have been available for a leading role in state, society, culture and management positions, highly qualified people with outstanding qualifications, including some icons of culture. The loss of human life had been over proportionate in those parts of the armed forces that required a high level of education and qualification, in particular the navy and air force, where up to eighty per cent of the manpower deployed perished that potentially should have been the new German elite. By contrast there were only minimal losses among those parts of the population that played a major part in oppressing 'the-good-ones', imposing the goals of the Nazis. Thus, during the period from 1945 to about 1968 the relevant deficits were apparent as was a preponderance of old Nazis in positions where they should not have been. This makes it almost a miracle that the implementation of the democratic state showed good progress.

Yet even today Germany still needs a renewal of its state and leadership culture. It needs people whose childhood, youth, adolescence and the educational phase has been engulfed in the spirit of Democracy. This may exist 'here-and-there' but is not the rule.

Building up a new leadership culture is a daunting task even at the best of times. Today's Germany is still struggling to find and emulate its appropriate priorities and the process may very well need much more time than has been envisaged. To have a true democratic spirit prevailing throughout all facets of the state you need some three consecutive generations of school children, university graduates, parents and teachers that have come through the ranks of a democratic environment. Whilst Britain, France and the United States can be called mature in this respect, Germany is just about scratching the surface, if you take 1945 and thereafter as starting date.

Germany has an additional problem. After the war, when Nazis were lying low, yielding the public arena to others, 'left-wingers' reached for the limelight, suggesting that Germany's cultural heritage was of the socialist or even communist persuasion. One of the slogans was *'der Geist steht links'*, meaning, freely, that the left was entitled to the high ground. This was mostly undisputed publicly as the 'right' *never* displayed any intellectual or cultural ambitions, preferring to make their mark by *other means*, whilst the silent majority of the population probably at all times and to this day never really cared one way or the other, preferring other playing fields outside the realm of public life and politics.

There is a small part of the population – I'll give them the label 'the good guys' - that is highly visible in a wide spectrum of public life, commerce, industry and the arts and culture but few in numbers and followers. Then there are those presumed to favour 'another camp', visible through highly conservative activities with a strong link to 'the-people' with all sorts of pageantry and traditionalism but no apparent dedication to the country. Politically they may even be the 'silent majority'. And somewhere there are the right-wing sympathizers, a segment of the population that is hard to quantify, preferring to choose their own privacy as and when it pleases them, only to make a big splash when it suits their hidden agendas. In a wider sense the bulk of the general public, often conspicuous as the self-declared, highly visible *Reiseweltmeister,* champion of world travel, hardly plays a part in German political life.

From these groups none clearly stands out as being the backbone of new elite. If I had to put my finger on it I would be hard pressed to say who and where the country's elite is today.

108

There is perhaps another argument that makes Germany different from many other countries. In the absence of a healthy 'middle' in Germany's post-war society the left as mentioned had claimed the high ground, accusing anyone seen as being to their right of being 'the establishment'. This not merely had an intellectual but also a social connotation, into which crept some rather ancient anti-capitalism with a touch of communism. The aristocracy had lost its innocence and the status of moral authority, as many of their members had joined the military – which traditionally always had been its role. Industrial circles were associated with war crimes and anybody economically better off was *per se* denied the moral right to be included in any elite. Thus even today, long after the Nazi period and the Third Reich, there appears to be no general recognition of the existence of *any* elite, a stratum of society to which I would attribute moral and intellectual leadership.

Any hint at 'elite' is quickly associated with material aspects, i.e. something the other fellow has and I have not. It's sad but an unpleasant reality.

So - does the country have elite?

I'd really like to know.

Entitlements

The German language has the word *Anspruch*, which brought out entitlement when I looked it up, wrongly, I think. Its meaning in German describes a right *per se*, something for which you have to do or give absolutely nothing in return. No matter what you do or not, it's yours. By contrast, if you own a piece of property you are entitled to some form of payment, if anybody wants to use it. If you come up with a hit-song you are entitled to royalties if anybody plays it. The point is that this English definition suggests something mutual like in give-and-take, more precisely: you give something and get something back. Not so in its German meaning. In a sense Anspruch reflects something that is typical for the authoritarian state. It is granted for free to make you happy so that you shut up and don't make trouble. And that is where this device came from: a seemingly generous gift to reconcile the blind followers, the subjects with the fact that the state treated them like a piece of garbage. It is really as cynical as that except that nowadays the government wants you to vote for them at the next election. Therefore they make it look nice.

An example helps: if you are the parent of a child you have *Anspruch* to *Kindergeld*. I won't translate this so as not to insult your linguistic faculties. All that is required is for the child to physically exist and that then triggers off the Anspruch. Don't get me wrong. Parents of young children should get all the help that is affordable. But such help should be embedded in a context where the recipient is required to do something in return. At least that should be coupled with your obligation to be a *good* parent or a *good* citizen and its disbursement should be contingent on need. I know that this puts me on the wrong side of some people but I let it stand. Our society thrives on mutuality - and there is an aspect of mutuality to be found in everything. If I have a child that goes to school and somebody gives me Kindergeld I should be able to find ample opportunity to give something back in return, a service, my time or my attention.

I can think of other situations where the German government would pay you without getting anything tangible in return other than that you do something that benefits you and nobody else, like fitting a new gadget to the exhaust system of your car, some kind of catalytic converter to clean up exhaust emissions. I find this quite odd. If fitting the converter is good for public health and welfare by leading to less emission you as a responsible citizen should get it as an obligation to society and the environment. If someone with a small income cannot afford it I'm sure one can find a way to help that person, a plausible way that compensates for the cost. I am objecting to the Anspruch *per se* for people to receive money for something they should do anyway and which in the long run is for their own good.

Then there is the situation where Anspruch comes closer to entitlement, e. g. in the context of employment contracts, where you are granted certain entitlements or rights. Some of these may be straightforward payment in kind as part of the employment contract; others may be intended to oblige you morally so that you love and want to continue working for that employer.

Generally speaking the citizen has so many cases of Anspruch that many think that it is best not to undertake *anything* unless the government grants you a certain Anspruch, i. e. promises you money for doing it, like insulating your house to cut down on your heating bills. This saves you money and the government pays you for it. From a business standpoint an investment that saves cost or generates income pays for itself so that there should be no need for a government handout, save for in the case of the needy.

In some ways that brings us back to Darwin. By paying the citizen for doing something that he would do anyway for his own good the government has stifled his enthusiasm for taking the initiative. If he waits long enough the government will pay him for doing it, hence, why bother. Many of the government handouts are little more than bribes to get votes at the next election. But some of these turn out to be very expensive as they keep on running indefinitely, well past the next election. Darwin comes in when you dispense with thinking what you can do and wait for the government instead.

Governments should not pay bribes when they can make demands, taking the citizen by honour and a sense of responsibility for the common good. A society has to find its way between these extremes:

- Everybody subjugates his own well-being to the common good, deriving his happiness from creating a happy state or

- Everybody places his own well-being first and grabs as much as he can get away with

The state should lead people to the realisation that they stand to benefit most when the state prospers. I am not aware that such thoughts have found their way into official thinking in Germany. This may be the right moment to quote John F. Kennedy:

> *Don't think what your country can do for you — think what you can do for your country.*

This also points to one of the weaknesses of today's Germany. Over the years the state has involved itself in so many aspects of individual well-being that it is hard to differentiate between essentials and luxuries on the one hand and public sector obligations and individual responsibility on the other. In broad principle the state should see to it that the citizen finds a level playing field that enhances his chances of sustainable and affordable employment instead of financing unemployment. In Germany this is a very sensitive issue.

Education

Education in Germany to me is a disaster area, marked by the lack of a modern, state-of-the-art, fair and equitable education system for the country in its entirety. Education by virtue of the Grundgesetz lies in the realm of state authority. Whilst the United States has one broad principle to establish the guidelines for education in its 50 states Germany has 16 different educational systems for 16 states. There has been a multitude of reforms but they just cannot come together, each one of them treating all the others like foreign countries. It would fill books to discuss the subject, but I want to keep the focus on the key issue: there exist differences between the 16 states but the common denominator on which they all converge is *injustice*.

If you want to understand a country, bring things down to basics: look at grade or elementary school. In the Anglo-Saxon inspired school or educational system and that of many countries which follow the same principles the consensus is that you want to reach people by way of reason and insight. This is the bread-and-butter-stuff of a democratic education: instil in people the conviction that it is best to do what is good for the country and society in the widest sense and that is ultimately for your own good. It creates the basis for living in an environment, in which you feel comfortable and makes you into a worthwhile member of that society. You give the children the possibility to explore their boundaries through trial-and-error, the fundamental educational principle that you can find practically everywhere in nature, to help that process along.

Except in Germany.

Education in Germany has its roots in authoritarian rule, which regulated human conduct by the principles of punishment and reward or the carrot and the stick, if you like. I avoided using the words 'German educational system' as such a thing does not exist. Germany is a federal republic made up of sixteen states, all of which have their own educational system and jurisdiction over it. One should have thought that since the early days of the Bundesrepublik creating a common school system would have been the number one priority. Sadly, it has not. There have been numerous reforms and efforts at interstate cooperation but there exists no unified school system, nor is there one in the making.

If you are a school teacher in one state, you may find it difficult to teach in another and your credentials acquired in another state may not be valid to teach there. Likewise you may find it frustrating as a student, if your parents move to another state, for you may have to find your way into a different system and get on top of it quickly or suffer the often severe disruptive consequences of falling behind, possibly losing a school year to get into step.

German school children are taught content, things to know, believe and learn. Matters have been evolving – to a point - and you do find attempts, based on good intentions, at breaking through the barrier of authoritarian teaching. But above all else stands the principle practically elevated to the state of dogma, that they want what's best for the child. And that is something that the child, left to his or her own devices, may never find unless being told where and how. They are afraid the child may get something wrong, make mistakes. Despite the odd hopeful sign here and there German education is run along the 'daddy-knows-best-approach'. The consequences of the German way of educating people have ramifications in practically all areas and significantly affect what goes on in the country. Hence its effects are a principal cause for concern.

Between childhood and grown-up working life at some stage we have to go through a process of education, meaning that at the end of it we should be suitably prepared and equipped to lead a useful life. We should be able to survive or do better through paid employment or other lawful means and raise a family, unless we are born filthy rich and stay that way. For the vast majority of us that means spending a few years attending school and subsequently learn a trade or go to university for suitable qualifications. Most countries have a school system that will facilitate choosing the appropriate education. Germany does not.

As mentioned, Germany does not have one school system but sixteen for as many states as there are. Whilst there may be similarities from one state school system to the other this is by no means intended. Education in Germany is the prerogative of the states and the federal government has no business getting involved. And the states will not be told!

114

All sixteen state school systems have their roots in the traditional German educational concept that goes back to the empire of the Kaiser and somehow came through the Weimar Republic and the Nazi era. Broadly speaking that system divides the children into two groups: a smaller one of people that after the initial four years of elementary school will go on to a secondary school, the Gymnasium or the Realschule, both of which offer the opportunity to pass the final exam, called Abitur. In the widest sense I would equate that with the American high school diploma, bearing in mind that an American high school combines under one roof what in Germany is parcelled out. The Abitur will allow you to go on to university or obtain qualifications in a wide variety of professions, for which it is the prerequisite.

By contrast, the part of children that are not singled out for secondary school have to stay in elementary school until the mandatory age, after which they may then try to find an apprenticeship with a private sector employer for vocational training, take up unskilled work, job-around, join a youth gang of some shady persuasion, including drugs and Nazi-party sympathizers or remain unemployed and try to live on social security.

If all goes well an apprenticeship should lead to a certificate called *Gesellenbrief*, a basic certificate of competence, documenting its successful completion, which is the prerequisite for numerous above average jobs in a working person's world. After that it leaves the option open to acquire the *Meisterbrief*, a crafts person's certificate of competence, Meister not to be confused with a master's at college. It is the highest you can go under normal circumstances, unless you qualify for and want to go on to one of the many polytechnic schools.

For the sake of social peace they are given the appearance of being universities and many try hard and succeed to come close to just that. It is an attempt at making good through the back-door a fundamental injustice that Germany is inflicting upon its youth by dividing them into people with or without the Abitur.

This division is based on an ancient and highly unfair class system that distinguishes between a seemingly brighter upper class, suitable for higher stations in life, and a majority confined to more lowly aims. Traditionally the latter were the people who would do the work or join the rank and file of the armed forces. The gap thus created runs through the fabric and fibre of the country's society and constitutes a rift that a person under normal circumstances cannot overcome during a lifetime. Once acquired it is there to stay. Abitur or not divides the country and leaves a stigma with those that don't have it.

This division seemingly on account of smartness or higher intelligence is complete nonsense and unsustainable on both scientific and humanitarian grounds, whilst being unworthy of a state that calls itself a Democracy with equal right for all. There are as many very smart people who are *not* given an opportunity to study for the Abitur and consequently have to stay way below their intellectual and occupational potential as there are certifiable idiots that somehow muddle through secondary education, make the Abitur and have plain sailing from there on.

The decision is made when the child is in fourth grade and teachers and/or parents decide whether the child stays in the elementary school or goes on into major league with Abitur, university and the rest. The determining factor in most cases is not intelligence or any special aptitude but the social background. If your father is a doctor you go on to Abitur, if he is an unskilled labourer you and your parents would have to fight like hell to go on. Basically the arbitrary division comprises two things: number one is a class prejudice that working class kids should be kept to themselves; the other is a prejudice expressed by many teachers that 'such-a-child-would-not-make-it' in the demanding environment of higher education. Admittedly learning Latin is harder if nobody in your family or surroundings has ever heard of Latin, but not impossible. Human beings have been known to rise to challenges if given the opportunity.

The German approach to school does not make it easy for intelligent and brilliant children from an immigrant background, mostly because often teachers take a small-minded view and think it will reflect badly on them if the kid subsequently does not make it in the secondary school system – for whatever reason. So they try to play it safe and persuade child and parents accordingly. That is an outrageous wrong and unjustifiable on any factual grounds. In the 1960s to early 1980s there was a great influx into the country of so called guest workers, initially from Italy, Spain and Greece and subsequently increasingly from Turkey to the effect that there now exists a segment of some three million people of Turkish descent and first generation ethnic Turks in the country.

With the third generation of people from an ethnic background reaching the schools we now know as hard fact that very often these children are better equipped to succeed. In addition to a high motivation they often come from a big-family background with an intact and well-functioning family structure and a high degree of supportiveness as well as self-motivation. As proof you now find people from a wide variety of countries that have established themselves in highly respected, solid positions in the country, people that are no longer immigrants but have arrived. Unfortunately, in public perception people of Turkish descent and German citizenship are often still referred to as 'Turks' when there really exists no necessity to even mention their ethnicity, or whatever it once was. There are the few that do break through the rigid divide in German education and more often than not come out on top of whatever they were aiming at, but they are too few and usually had to work unduly hard for it.

Of course, there have been many attempts at state level to bring about meaningful reforms but all of them failed to identify and as a consequence address the key issue: most such attempts confused 'equal-treatment-for-all' with 'equal-fair-chances-and-opportunities-for-all'. In broad principle all German attempts at educational reform are based on the principle of grouping a number of people together in accordance with certain selection criteria, all of which then have to do the same; it is maddening but they always think in terms of 'groups', not 'individuals'. My totally unproven and unscientific idea is that the absolute state wanted to control people; and it is so much easier to control groups than numbers of individuals.

This may be the appropriate moment to point towards the American school system, which really *is* a system, although every little school has certain freedoms to do its own thing. Its importance is that it offers equal opportunity. If you want to get ahead in the American school system you will find a way and there will be many elements to help you. In the long run, school is not about acquiring knowledge, as the Germans mistakenly believe: it is about discovering who you are as an individual and what your strengths and weaknesses are and how best to develop and if need be work around them towards achieving objectives. The German alternative is to match situations that we encounter with blueprints of solutions stored in our memory banks.

Education starts in kindergarten, not high school or university. In America children in kindergarten may pick up a snippet of knowledge that someday they may become president of the United States. Good kindergarten education implants friendly visions to aspire to and provides some rather basic orientation and guidance. In what used to be West Germany a significant part of small children do *not* go to kindergarten as the state or the communities do not provide a suitable system for all. The situation was significantly better in East Germany during the times of the GDR but most of it was scuttled, often as 'economically non-viable' but maybe often more likely on ideological grounds as being a remnant from the socialist era. But they did have one or two good things in the GDR.

If I had to put it in a nutshell I would say that the American view on kindergarten is to kindle self-motivation, enthusiasm for learning and a certain degree of self-management and social competence whilst in Germany the buzz words are 'good behaviour' and 'discipline', which more or less gives two names for the same thing but signals falling short of developing a child's personality and potential.

Germany has some youth unemployment and untrained and un-educated youth, whilst many bosses in industry clamour for attracting skilled personnel from abroad. During the early stages of my professional career I repeatedly worked alongside colleagues in former British colonies from whom I learned that 'there are no bad soldiers but only bad officers', meaning that we have to be prepared to invest in educating and training the people we want to work with and help them to bring out their potential.

The Germans on the whole prefer to cut short on that part, saving themselves both the cost and the trouble of providing adequate training in exchange for 'buying-in' the finished product that was generated through the often limited resources of a country on the road to further development. Effectively this is a case of reverse or retro-development aid with the highly developed industrial country, Germany, being the recipient and beneficiary of subsidies at the expense of a nation in the course of development, depriving such nations of the benefits to be derived from the work in their own country by people for whose education they paid.

Looking at the large numbers of young people in Germany to whom fair chances for an adequate education are not extended it appears absurd that German industry is clamouring that there are not enough sufficiently qualified people for the workforce, demanding recruiting campaigns of fully educated and trained people from abroad under a number of so-called 'green-card' incentives that have been proposed.

The Germans proudly point towards their low level of youth unemployment, which they attribute partly to their dual-system, called *Duales System*, whereby young people receive their vocational training through hands-on employment in industry. The Germans state that their dual system leads to less youth unemployment compared to a vocational training program as part of national education, which they call *'ein verschultes System'*. This in my eyes is no more and no less than an enormous scandal, which results from a remnant of Germany's authoritarian if not outright feudal traditions.

The German way prematurely curbs educational opportunities of young people before their real potential becomes apparent. It is grossly unfair in that it denies the full scope of opportunities to those that are rather randomly eliminated from joining the country's future elite by a spot-decision at age ten or thereabouts. Those kept out of the secondary school system are left on their own, whilst secondary education is the responsibility of the state. Those left out are often the children of migrants from abroad or low-income families. It is possible to break through this unfair system if one can generate enough of an effort. But if the parents are immigrants without a sufficient command of the German language chances of success are minimal. At any rate, the German dual-system unfairly favours those that already have a secure base to the detriment of those that really need to gain a foothold in the country's economy and society, above all fair treatment and an equal chance.

Whilst France seemingly has a militant workforce the Germans appear rather meek and docile, making Germany into a country with a 'good' labour climate. That is deceptive. In reality the French stand up for and defend their rights whilst the Germans are being curbed through complicity of unions and industry, which benefits capital interests to the detriment of the national economy. Capital interests obtain an advantage through cost reduction whilst its consequences through unemployment and reduced domestic levels of activity are nationalised, as a burden of the state.

On a European scale the problem lies in the fact that internationally there exist no suitable programs to lead young people into employment on finishing school, whilst German industry snaps up their apprentices as cheap labour that may subsequently become grown-up unemployed. This would be avoided if Europe for once lends a helping hand in setting the scales right and creates grassroots fairness throughout all of Europe. After all, if the European Union can regulate the curvature of cucumbers or bananas I do not see why they could not set fair guidelines for starting young people in working life to fair and equitable standards throughout all of Europe in such a way that everybody finds equal, fair and acceptable starting conditions.

Let me try to wrap up this point. Education in Germany had its roots in the absolute or authoritarian state with lots of help from the Church. Ever since the early days of the federal republic there have been numerous attempts at reform that to the best of my knowledge and - more appropriately – in my opinion have not resulted in the existence of a satisfactory system. These are my key points of contention:

1. The German approach emphasises the acquisition of knowledge rather than gaining insights and fundamental, broad understanding

2. There exists very little if any understanding of the importance of trial-and-error to enable children to find their own way and discover their potential

3. Education sets in too late, usually after a child's sixth birthday rather than as and when the child is ready for going to school

4. It is too rigid

5. It is overloaded with ideologically motivated and otherwise unnecessary elements

6. Education to university level takes too long

7. It does not sufficiently take into account a person's natural dispositions, skills and aptitudes, requiring groups of people to do the same thing with no individual differentiation

8. It is totally un-democratic with regards to the issue of whether or not a child should find an open road towards acquiring the Abitur, effectively access to wider education opportunities

9. By consequence it is totally un-democratic by not providing equal opportunities for all, obliging those that do not head for the Abitur to seek on their own initiative and at their own expense private sector vocational training

10. It is totally un-democratic towards children with special needs that should have the same right as everybody else in the country to a complete education; they are often relegated to a back-corner, away from public attention and confined to 'special' schools outside the general school system and mostly with very limited resources at their disposal and consequently limited scope and perspective

These last three points are not in accordance with the vision of equal rights for all. At first I thought that the German constitution grants equal rights for all. When looking for a relevant clause I could not find it . . . until I looked it up in the American constitution, where of course I did finds it – as if I hadn't remembered it from high school.

Did the Germans overlook this point?

Law and Order and the Legal System

It is a generally accepted principle that modern countries, their society, the business community and government institutions should be embedded in an environment of ordered and lawful processes, the functioning of which is transparent, readily accessible and affordable and over-all just. Whilst the casual onlooker might have the notion that things are more or less the same in all countries nothing could be further from the truth. In actual practice the various countries each have their own specific legal and law enforcement environment that has evolved with the country's history, its traditions and its heart and soul that injects life into an otherwise dry matter. The latter point is the human factor that determines whether we hate it, suffer through or feel good in a country. Ideally we want the latter and like to label anything less on a sliding scale from 'go-there-if-you-must' to 'avoid'. I can still remember that during the time of the Iron Curtain the mere thought of going to one of those countries would cause a mixture of chills and high blood-pressure.

Traditionally legal systems in Europe owe a lot to a few principles that have remained valid to this day, which go back to ancient Roman civilisation; in America you sometimes get the impression that you have to be fluent in Latin to understand half of what the lawyers are saying. To me the era of Napoleon marks a big leap forward. He introduced the Code Napoléon from which evolved the French Code Civil as useful and practical tools for the advancement of trade and industry, providing clear and easily understandable guidance. We refer to it as codified law, setting out the relevant rules and points of law to follow and the punishment that awaits you if you don't. It is a bit like a catalogue of what you can get away with.

The English have gone down a totally different route with their Case Law that remains in effect to this day. It is sometimes also referred to as 'unwritten law' as there exists no codified law book. Save for matters that have been dealt with in specific legislation each situation is considered on the grounds of its merits and shortcomings and court cases often explore precedents of earlier rulings under similar or near identical circumstances. Some say it is complicated and cumbersome and its processes, involving research into case histories, are time consuming and expensive, but it has one huge advantage over the written, codified approach. Each case is looked at individually und ultimately decided by the purest of all legal systems: the wisdom of an enlightened judge or jury – in theory, that is.

The Germans opted for the codified approach. Probably inspired by the Code Napoléon the new German empire at an early stage passed into law a comprehensive codified legal work that received a lot of praise for its thoroughness, transparency and ease of implementation in daily life, business and legal cases. In German it is comprehensively referred to as *Deutsches Recht*, German Law. Its backbone is the *Buergerliches Gesetzbuch*, short BGB, which translates freely into the citizens' law book. The code is actually made up of a number of individual books that deal with the various legal aspects from civil matters to trade, industry, labour law and penal code. Its thoroughness is impressive: you name it, they have it. One of the drawbacks of codified law is the fact that it reflects the legal consensus that prevailed at the time of its inception and under the specific circumstances on which its rulings are based, which means that in due course the need will arise to adjust or update it.

The problem lies in finding the right moment as to when any updates or changes should be incorporated so that the legal system remains in step with the advancement of society, business practices and state philosophies. That is precisely its biggest drawback. The longer it has been in effect the more it has led to rigidity in legal matters, to the point that increasingly the letter of the law has become more important than the substance that lies behind it and only too often legal form triumphs over content matter. In actual practice that may lead to court decisions that may seem unjust but are in strict accordance with the book.

After the formation of the Federal Republic German society made a big leap forward in shaking off constraints that through its underlying authoritarian state philosophy were reflected in German law. A steadily growing high level of general discontent of citizens with their state erupted in the student riots of 1968. In its wake much of that which had been contentious in the law books was rectified, but not all. That which has remained to this day is the rigidity with which it is applied. Let us not forget that it had its origins in the authoritarian spirit that ruled during the period of its inception, which was based on 'control' rather than 'trust'. This has locked the legal process into a very cold environment and to a great extent de-humanised it.

With regards to legal matters in the widest sense the Germans cling to the letter of the law. Take the example of civil disobedience for acceptable good reasons, acting outside the envelope of 'written law' as found in the volumes of the official German law books. If today you do something very courageous with a positive outcome but not in strict compliance with the provisions of the relevant legal stipulations you may still have to answer charges. The courts may then bend over backwards to exculpate you on the grounds of 'particular circumstances' but will uphold the legal points that you violated, instead of coming right out to say: look, here is a brave man, and then drop any charges. They don't feel comfortable unless they have gone through the whole formal procedure, even if the outcome is predictable.

There are countless cases of 'good-Samaritans' that were sentenced for what the German legal system calls *Handlung ohne Auftrag*, acting without due authorisation and you may have to bear the consequences. The Germans know that and think twice before engaging in acts of outstanding bravery. The German legal system stifles good citizenship that is not based on the all-clear by your lawyer – overstated but always there in spirit. Where others may judge you on nobility of spirit the Germans will hold you to the letter of the law, a law that may have been conceived in the cultural and legal environment of, say, a hundred years ago.

In recent years the Bundestag, the federal parliament, has been producing new laws at an accelerated pace. Increasingly this is an encumbrance, stifling the advancement and development of the country. Much new legislation has been hastily put together, often seeking to impress the public so as to convey the feeling 'that-the-government-is-actually-doing-something'.

The existing German legal culture obliges the courts to produce rulings that are compatible with the letter of the law. There is not really much room for civil courage and departing from any obsolescent pieces of law that may come to light. This can be frustrating. The principle of codified law entails the risk that the more it goes into detail the more gaps and loopholes it opens up. This could easily be rectified if the law were handled less rigidly, opening up a wider margin for individual consideration of circumstances. But that is next to impossible to achieve when the overriding principle is the maintenance of Ordnung that we discussed earlier.

In broad principle the German legal system is workable but it would benefit enormously from a bit more sunshine. By that I mean that very detailed codified law can be a curse if left in the hands of people that are in actual fact bean-counters, striving for *perfection* up to the finest detail. In some ways the Germans tend to make themselves the prisoners of their own system. Sometimes they trip over their own feet, afraid to give it a good shake-up. There are situations in life when things boil down to 'no guts – no glory', when you have to do something that is right but not in the law book. Maybe this is one of the rare points where the Church could help with the old maxim of *pecca fortiter!* which translates freely into: if you have to sin, do so with courage!

Only death offers ultimate perfection. If you opt for life you have to learn to live with imperfection. Perhaps the Germans should relax a bit more - then all will be fine.

The State Official

Governments since ancient times have relied on people in their service to project power to even the remotest parts of the country. We usually speak of government officials but in the case of Germany I would like to call them 'state officials', by which I draw attention to the fact that in Germany things are different: there are two types of government employee, one called 'Beamter', which I want to translate as *state official* and the other, the 'Angestellte', being *state employee*. The latter has the same status of employee as is common for employment in normal business, whilst the state official has his job for life, cannot be fired and has to abide by a code of conduct as stipulated in the *Beamtenrecht*, translated freely as terms and conditions of employment as state official. In addition to having a safe job for their entire working life and a nice pension when it is over they enjoy numerous perks and privileges, enhancing their material position, like a cosy health insurance system, housing and transportation allowances and access to buying certain goods at wholesale prices.

Of course they owe their employer absolute loyalty, which goes without saying. In addition they must not engage in any activity or do anything in the course of the discharge of their duties that results in any material damages, financial obligations or loss for the state arising out of their activities. Broadly speaking, they must not come into conflict with the code of conduct, the Beamtenrecht. If they do they lose their privileges and perks forthwith and the job on top of it. That is as tough as it sounds – a bit like always working with a gun pointed at your head. What originally may have been a good idea has turned into an encumbrance of the whole system of having state officials at all.

In many cases the state official is the kingpin of government contracts; in the drawing up, letting and administering of goods, supplies or services. Even if the state official carries out his work to perfection and under the best of circumstances that entails risks, which may result in losses or claims for damages. He is effectively in a 'no-mistake-position' and 'if he makes it', in a manner of speaking, he may be sacked. A successful state official can be defined as one that reaches the fruits of his labours safely, his pension.

Government projects are audited. If it transpires that a project incurs a cost overrun that the state official should have foreseen and did not, he may be held liable: found to have acted against his terms and conditions of contract. There is a certain tolerance for errors or mistakes but it is minimal. As a consequence he will shy away from anything that entails even the slightest risk and financial claims potential. Instead he will see to it that all his actions will protect him and his employer, the state, from losses or claims.

He achieves this by farming out the decision-making process to outside advisors or experts. It is commonly accepted procedure that his backside will be covered, as long as he goes for what is known as 'a big name', a well-known company or individual. If subsequently losses are incurred because *they* made a mistake that is simply 'tough luck' and will not be held against him. By appointing a big name he did what was expected of him, 'playing it safe'.

This has consequences for the state: we have come to accept that our business world thrives on sustained 'process improvement', which means that the more you do the better at it you become, due to the benefits and blessings of trial-and-error.

The state official is barred from incurring errors, which means that trial-and-error for him is not an option; he has no other choice than to go out-of-house for the assignment, appoint an expert or a company.

As a consequence any advancement on the learning curve accrues to the expert, not the state official or consequently his employer, the state.

Thus the state may make the same mistake fifteen dozen times in a row without hope of improvement through a learning process. In case you wonder why nobody changes this situation so do I, for it would be ridiculously easy to do. All you have to do is remove some of the archaic perks and privileges in exchange for absolving the state official, once and for all, from any claims against the state, for which he may be held responsible, save for cases of criminal or malicious neglect and all the usual provisos like fraud or theft, for which an ordinary mortal is accountable anyway. For the state official that would mean giving up a certain degree of comfort and security but he would also get rid of the pressure. For the state that would mean a quantum leap forward.

The ambient atmosphere of a state lies somewhere between totally authoritarian to absolutely democratic. You can glean the position it has reached from the prevalence of state officials. As we know the United States is managing quite well *without any* state officials at all and has done so from day one. Germany inherited the system of state officials from its predecessor state, the Third Reich or Nazi Germany, which in turn inherited it from the Kaiser's empire. For both regimes it made sense to have state officials that would carry out orders blindly and to the letter and we know why and to what end.

In Democracy there is neither a place nor the need for them.

Fundamental Rights vs. State Supremacy

We have come to one of the 'big-points', in a manner of speaking. We need to look at something so essential, that it stands above opinion, points of view or interpretation: fundamental rights. I said elsewhere in this script that they are more or less laid down in the ten commandments of the Christian Bible and most people will probably agree.

Always?

Well. It appears that sometimes they do not. We learn that we should not steal, but some Germans, including some in government, think that stealing is perfectly all right if it benefits the state. People have been illegally copying confidential bank files and selling them to the German government, either at state or federal level. These files are records of deposits made in foreign banks outside Germany that, when checked against official German tax records, reveal that tax evasion has taken place, i.e. people channelled undeclared income, taxable in Germany, into a bank account abroad, hidden from the beady eye of the German taxman.

The relevant data were obtained without the consent of the bank or the account holder and thus obtained illegally: in plain English the word is *stolen* and the process of their acquisition is commonly referred to as *theft*. It has been revealed that some such data were used in court cases whereby the government has been suing the account holders and penalising them if found guilty. Rumour has it that it washed 'millions' into official German coffers.

Under German law as well as that of many other civilised countries it is a crime to sell or buy stolen goods. The process of doing it anyway is commonly referred to as *fencing*. When cases of stolen or illegally obtained CDs containing bank data became known, surprisingly for me, there was wide-spread approval of how the matter was handled, buying the stolen discs and using the data as evidence in court cases to prosecute tax-dodgers. The debate ran along the following lines:

The Fundamental Rights vs. Stolen Discs Debate

Public Opinion PO: "The CDs with the data revealed funds for which the appropriate tax had not been paid."

Concerned Citizen CC: "The CDs with the data had been stolen."

PO: "Under German law tax evasion is punishable."

CC: "So is stealing."

PO: "The government did not steal the CDs but bought them."

CC: "Buying stolen goods is also against the law."

PO: "But it was to a good end, serving the common good."

CC: "So the – criminal – means of stealing are justified by the end?"

PO: "Yeah, why not?"

CC: "Because that is like the old *'l'état c'est moi!'* I am the state, meaning that as long as it is good for the state that's all right".

PO: "You have to set priorities. Morally the people depositing their money abroad had been doing wrong by evading the payment of taxes and the state has now put it right. How else should the state have done it?"

CC: "The state should have set up a fair tax system and educated its citizens that it is for the common good to pay one's taxes."

PO: "Some people just will not listen to reasoning and don't have the necessary insight. They need to get their backsides kicked in!"

CC: "And who decides when that is OK?"

PO: "The courts."

CC: "And the stealing and fencing of the data is not prosecuted?"

PO: "That served the common good."

CC: "That is immoral."

PO: "Grow up, man! Live in the real world. The state got its taxes which the taxpayers had evaded."

CC: "So we have laws against stealing and fencing but they do not apply to the state?"

PO: "Not paying the tax was the greater wrong."

CC: "Yeah, the old Machiavellian approach."

We can leave it here, for the debate will just continue to go around in circles. There are other examples worth looking into. For forty years East and West Germany existed alongside each other as separate, independently functioning entities, had their own laws, institutions and state sovereignty. The West Germans dealt with the East Germans *de facto*, not *de jure*, which means they did not recognise the East German GDR as a state but traded with them vigorously and did a lot of things that states do between each other.

By our definitions the GDR was a totalitarian state that forbade its citizens to leave the country, save for with state's permission. This was mostly not readily given. Over time, in search of freedom and attracted by the West's better living conditions some two million out of the GDR's total population of about eighteen million fled the country, many to West Germany. To stop this the GDR built the Berlin Wall, fortified the border with West Germany and went as far as authorising border guards to shoot people that tried to leave the country illegally. Over time this resulted in numerous deaths.

After German unification West German and subsequently the new all-German authorities brought court cases against East German border guards that had been involved in shooting incidents, their superiors and the state politicians above them in the chain of command, many of which were sent to jail.

Of course shooting unarmed civilians that tried to struggle through barbed-wire fences, threatened by ferocious dogs and mine-fields was quite terrible: It was a very nasty and repugnant thing. However, the GDR was a sovereign state. Sovereign states have rights and one of them is the defence of their borders, whether that pleases people or not. Under their laws these actions were ordered by their state and people in the chain of command had to carry them out, no ifs and buts. Morality is one thing but the West Germans traded vigorously with the GDR and had no moral hang-ups doing that, thereby *de facto* recognising the regime.

What is objectionable is the fact that West German courts retro-actively made West German law legally binding on the East

Germans. That practice is referred to as *ex-post-facto jurisdiction*, which we do not condone in the civilised West. I am not aware of any significant criticism of these court rulings coming out of West Germany. Quite the opposite!

West Germans generally accepted that former East German officials were prosecuted for alleged 'Berlin-Wall' and 'Iron-Curtain' crimes, as they were commonly referred to. There lies a certain high-handedness in how the German legal profession through its rank and file is prepared to disregard own laws in pursuing interests of the state and extend German jurisdiction abroad – albeit temporarily and if it suits them. But that is not democratic – it is authoritarian.

To those that want to cite the American example let me say that the United States *has* passed legislation that is binding *world-wide* on its own citizens and institutions, but that is a totally different story, because the US has jurisdiction over them. In the case of the GDR West Germany did not have jurisdiction – they just claimed they did, retro-actively.

With complete sincerity Germany wants to be a democracy. Germany still has its work cut out for it, if in the process of becoming an accomplished democracy you think of requiring three consecutive generations of *bona fide* democrats. It takes patience, prudence, enlightenment and commitment. It is long-haul, not quick gains. There are primarily these points that still require appropriate action:

- The country's school system needs to be embedded in actively lived, not lectured down democracy from kindergarten upwards, restructured to offer equal rights and standards for all; academic and vocational goals have to be equally respected and children from ethnic backgrounds and with special needs need to be given fair treatment and an equal place in the system

- The German legal system and culture need to be reconciled with the prerequisites of Democracy; fundamental rights have to be placed above formal procedures, not vice-versa as is today's practice

- Public life, the guidelines of public and private conduct and the relationship between citizen and state have to be lifted out of an environment of distrust and suspicion and reconciled with the preamble of the country's constitution, which stipulates that human dignity is untouchable and indivisible - not just 'in the book' but practiced top to bottom in daily life

Germany has to deal with these points. They stand in the way of according them the respect and recognition they desire. Everything else will fall into place, once these points have been dealt with appropriately. After all, Germany is still a young democracy.

I said it before and I'll say it again: freedom and democracy are two sides to a coin — one cannot exist without the other. Two thousand years of authoritarian rule have stood in the way of freedom. Give it time. The Germans will get there. They are a good people and they have the integrity and sincerity to persevere. At least that is my hope.

The Road to Disaster

Someone probing into recent German history with two horrendous wars and one of the bloodiest tyrannies in human memory is bound to arrive at these questions:

How was all this possible?

Can it happen again?

Compelled by what I call my 'mature gut feeling' I want to say without hesitation: not imperial Germany and not a scenario that made the country one of the principal protagonists of World Wars I and II. But this response is in some ways conditional and implies reservations. We may have to dig deeper.

The burning question is: what made Hitler and the Third Reich, the Nazi state, possible? Not many occurrences in history have been more thoroughly and meticulously researched and explored than those surrounding the Third Reich and what led up to it. We have the findings and utterances of numerous sources: scholars, historians, scientists, politicians and perfectly ordinary people, in their entirety dedicated to a full understanding of a very complex scenario, thereby hoping to encompass it adequately. Despite all the scholarly brilliance of those involved there may be an aspect or two that has not yet been brought out into the open. At the heart of it all there are a number of at first seemingly unrelated events or circumstances, all converging as if with diabolical precision and evil pre-determination on bringing Adolf Hitler to power as chancellor of the German Republic. Today historians agree that these three main strands stand out in particular among the factors that helped Hitler rise to power:

- Resentment of the circumstances surrounding the end of World War I

- Growing general disenchantment with the Weimar Republic and what it stood for and

- The rise in popularity and acceptance of Hitler and his NSDAP Nazi party at an ever quickening pace since the late 1920s

Subconsciously for most these points were strung together. For some, in particular the monarchists, the totally unfamiliar concept

134

of democratic government seemed unacceptable. Being widely split into factions that opposed one another over policy issues they ultimately concurred, after some hesitation, in seeing Hitler as a figure that they could use to get rid of the republic, the unloved successor to the empire. They had an agenda of their own.

But when it comes to the crunch a great number of people felt resentment over the shameful end to the war, World War I, seeing Hitler as the knight in shining armour that could restore their self-esteem. Hitler was growing into hero-status with an aura of infallibility, to which he himself bluntly added the suggestion that he may have been sent by what he called *Die Vorsehung*, a word which he himself may have created and for which there does not really exist a time-honoured translation into English. But the meaning was clear: God-given, by which he capitalised on the old myth of God-given authority that had been prevailing in Germanic lands and for which none other than Martin Luther may have to accept some responsibility.

Thus in the period referred to as that of the Weimar Republic (1918-1933), engulfed in an atmosphere of turmoil and uncertainty, the foundation of the Third Reich, the Nazi-fascist totalitarian state (1933-1945), was laid by Hitler and his followers with determination and vigour, helped inadvertently if not by default by the rest of the country, ultimately and unavoidably leading up to a cruel dictatorship, the holocaust, World War II and a great void at its end, into which was to slip a new German state, the Federal Republic of Germany of today.

But one step at a time.

At the end of World War I it would not have been possible to predict any of all that with an adequate degree of certainty and yet it happened. From seemingly unspectacular beginnings a synergetic process was set in motion that first became increasingly and then absolutely unstoppable and irreversible.

On 30 January 1933 the German president, Reichspräsident Hindenburg, installed Hitler in the position of Reichskanzler, chancellor of the Reich, i.e. effectively prime minister of what then still was the German Republic, commonly referred to as the Weimar Republic. National elections held soon thereafter on 05 March 1933 had Hitler's party, the NSDAP, at no more than 43.9%, still a far cry from the expected majority, which Hitler was not to attain until well *after* he had already consolidated his grip on the country.

There would have been a ray of hope for Democracy, had there been any strong enough alliance to stand in the way of Hitler. About a third of voters were still supporting the parties that upheld the Weimar Republic, namely SPD, DDP and Zentrum with a total of 30.4% of the vote and the communist KPD making up he balance to Hitler's NSDAP. Alas that which Hitler called *Die Vorsehung,* that mysterious voice-from-above or the hand of fate thought otherwise. Those that could have stopped him, had they been united, bitterly opposed one another.

Once he was chancellor he formed a coalition government with the monarchists, represented by the Deutsche Nationale Volkspartei DNVP and reluctantly on their part the Deutsche Staatspartei DDP. Only some five months later, on 27 June 1933, the DNVP, and one day thereafter the DDP, which had helped Hitler's NSDAP to gain a parliamentary majority, 'decided to disband voluntarily'. In clear language that means they were forced to do so.In this they were followed by the Catholic Zentrum on 05 July 1933, which also disbanded, of course under pressure. On 22 June 1933; the socialist SPD had already been banned by decree and on 26 June 1933 the assets of the Communist Party had been confiscated and the party banned. Under the terms of the constitution of the Weimar Republic these thereby perfectly legal measures left Hitler's NSDAP as the only remaining political party in parliament.

It had taken less than thirty weeks to turn the country irreversibly from a democracy into a dictatorship and all this by formally correct legal means.

President Hindenburg unwittingly had gone a long way towards preparing the ground for Hitler's rise to absolute power. We may doubt whether he was fully aware of that. On 04 and 28 February 1933 Hindenburg issued two legal documents that limited parliamentary control whilst creating an instrument for government by decree. This had been prompted by the fear of street terror with the risk of washing power into the wrong hands. Had he only known or anticipated what was to come! These were the legal instruments that Hitler in his capacity as chancellor used to abolish his opposition and thereby also Democracy.

The first of these measures had been a reaction to general street terror by various groups. The second one was the direct response to an arson attempt on the building of the *Reichstag* on 27 February 1933. Without producing conclusive proof some later suggested that the Nazis had laid fire. Whatever was the truth, basic rights were curbed and those for government by decree strengthened. These two measures were reinforced by a third, the most definitive one, the *Ermächtigungsgesetz,* the Empowerment Act, which enabled the government, effectively the president and the chancellor, to ban or regulate practically everything, abolishing political parties, the freedom of the press and a whole host of other measures. The third and most definitive one of these acts of legislation was passed by majority vote of the Reichstag, which means of course that it was *legal.* Now all the tools were lined up and in place for a legal transfer of power into the hands of Hitler, come the right moment.

At this point a look at the political parties may be useful to explain how things were connected. Out of the political debris of the failed empire two entirely new parties had emerged: *The nationalsozialistische deutsche Arbeiterpartei,* the National Socialist German Workers' Party, short NSDAP, and the *Deutsche kommunistische Partei,* the Communists, short KPD. Both had as their objective creating a dictatorship, albeit each dedicated to its own particular set of prerogatives, none of which contained any allusions to democratic government nor had either one of these two any common grounds with the other two mainstream parties, the Sozialdemokraten, social Democrats, short SPD, and the monarchists that considered themselves to be the rightful successors to that which the empire had stood for. They were the DNVP and the DDP already mentioned, rather diffuse entities with no clear leadership and ramifications branching off in several directions. For them any alliance with either NSDAP or KPD had been completely out of the question, which had left the political scene split broadly into three main blocs: the right and left wing radicals and the more moderate democratically inclined parties, to which has to be added the small Zentrumspartei or Zentrum (originally spelled Centrum), which meant to uphold primarily Catholic values. This had left German parliamentary politics wide open as a disputed battleground, as none of these three blocks on its own would be able to command a parliamentary majority. The scales tipped when DNVP and DDP each on its own abandoning an earlier stand had drifted towards the NSDAP, only to discover that you may wind up as the main dish if you go on a picnic with a monster.

After the end of the empire and the invocation of the republic the monarchists, the DNVP and the DVP, had hoped to be able to get back into power, resisted by the democrats, being SPD, DDP and Zentrum. Their confidence was partly based on the provisions of the Weimar constitution with sweeping powers in the hands of the president, into which office they had helped elect a succession of staunch monarchists, the last of them Hindenburg,

This sadly may have been the last nail in the coffin of Democracy inasmuch as the Weimar Republic was concerned. On 02 August 1934 Hindenburg died at the age of 86. Rather than go for a successor Hitler proposed to merge the offices of president and chancellor, combining the already limitless powers of both in the newly created position of *Führer und Reichskanzler*. Confident of having gained full public acceptance Hitler put this measure up for vote by the public. In a referendum held on 19 August 1934 of an electorate of 95% of eligible voters 89% voted in favour, by which measure Hitler became Hindenburg's successor, duly elected by the German people with public acceptance beyond the shadow of doubt.

Hitler had become Führer – legally.

All the time having dodged around the issue of dealing with the country's armed forces, the Reichswehr, he now, all of a sudden, had become their commander-in-chief, which settled the argument with undisputed clarity. This only leaves to mention that Hitler and his followers lost no time to give the country a 'wall-to-wall-Nazi-infrastructure', covering every aspect that you could think of, making Germany into a totally Nazi-dominated fascist state.

Hitler, the man himself, had now become the German government, combining in his person all legislative, executive and judicial powers, commander-in-chief of the armed forces and the country's Führer, entitled to everybody's obedience, if not blind faith - to the death. What might have been hard if not impossible to achieve through political struggle, short of armed uprising and revolution, had fallen into Hitler's lap, made possible by the country's constitution and the public spirit and feeling prevailing at the time. This had been enhanced by his demonic charisma and Nazi street violence had done the rest when it was useful to make people crave peace and stability. And in the background — not to be taken lightly — there was the country's dark heritage.

The monarchists had tried to use the Nazis, double-crossing them for their own objectives, but Hitler turned that around into double crossing the monarchists that had helped him into power, the classic double-double-cross.

Recently I came across a comment that referred to the entire period from 1914 to 1945 as one single, contiguous sad and tragic disaster rather than a sequence of two or several seemingly individual or even isolated events. The idea is by no means new that World War II was an attempt to settle, once and for all, issues that had first been allowed to arise out of an inadequate end to its predecessor and then spiralled out of control. But that applied primarily to the German side of the argument whilst the victors of World War I would have happily closed the case for good and moved on.

At the time of the outbreak of World War I the German Empire was looking back on a history of no more than 43 years since its proclamation. The Germans had just beaten the French forces in the Battle of Sedan and taken prisoner French Emperor Napoleon III. On 18 January 1871 led by the Kingdom of Prussia the victorious Germans had chosen the hallowed halls of the Chateau de Versailles, a venue on French soil, for the act of victory celebration, elevated with great pomp to the launch of the new German Empire. This was marked by a very spectacular and highly emotional proclamation. Into the newly created German Empire were inducted the various extant German political entities that had been loosely associated in the *Deutscher Bund*, the German Confederation, and aligned other territories, comprising the four kingdoms of Prussia, Bavaria, Württemberg and Saxony, ten dukedoms, eight principalities, the three free cities of Hamburg, Bremen and Lübeck and the territory of Alsace-Lorraine, originally merged into France in the Napoleonic Wars and usurped by the new empire as part of the spoils of war. It should be noted that those behind the formation of the Empire did all that was in their earthly powers to leave outside Austria. The Prussians wanted to be number one and Austria did not fit into such plans.

The various German political entities had been lured if not co-erced into the German-French conflict. It had had very little to do with compelling genuine German issues and had been brought about, engineered and masterminded by Chancellor Bismarck of the Kingdom of Prussia with the intent of giving the various German nobles and principals something around which they could rally and which in the euphoria of military victory would carry them to elevate one from within their midst to German Emperor, Prussian King Wilhelm Friedrich to become Kaiser Wilhelm, the first emperor of the new German Empire. The *casus belli*, the pretext for going to war, had been dissent over the question of succession to the Spanish throne, not exactly a burning issue from the German standpoint, which Bismarck had craftily used to stir up emotions by first falsifying and then 'falsely rectifying' salient information and its representation in the press.

By international standards the proclamation on foreign soil of a new empire would be an outrage today and it was an outrage then. It was the kind of action that was guaranteed to breed deep resentment, even hate, for years if not generations to come. Here was an upstart, hodgepodge battlefield association that had dared invade the territory of an established nation state, using the occasion to the fullest to humiliate their victims. This was bound to leave a deep wound in French heart and soul that would cry out for no less than one ultimate remedy and satisfaction: revenge.

That may explain the attitude with which 47 years later the French along with their allies of World War I treated the German representatives, surrendering to the victorious French military commanders and those of their allies: contempt. As a fitting anti-climax and to rub in the magnitude of the lowest possible choice of protocol whilst delivering the revenge on French soil a railway carriage was chosen as venue as a stark contrast to the spectacle of 1871 at the Chateau de Versailles, marking with something of a hammer-blow the inglorious end of what was perhaps the shortest-lived empire, ever.

During the period preceding World War I German Kaiser Wilhelm II and his government had hardly missed an opportunity to cause indignation on the international scene, be it the highly inappropriate meddling of the Germans against the British in the Boer War, highlighted by the ill-advised 'Krueger-Telegram', congratulating the Boers of South Africa on their insurrection against the Brit-

140

ish or gunboat diplomacy in North Africa, highlighted by the equally ill-advised 'Leap-of-the-Panther' gunboat excursion to Agadir in North Africa of 1911, trying to exert pressure on the French over the question of colonies. It derived its name from the German gunboat SMS Panther, sent onto the scene on the occasion.

Both efforts not merely failed from the German point of view but served to drive together the French and the British to form their *entente cordiale*, a defensive alliance, in due course to be joined by the Russians, to safeguard against any German threat. For this the term *encirclement* came into fashion, marking the total isolation of Germany. The Germans had not been out to win international popularity contests. Nationalism was up in the air. The Germans had wanted their moments of fame. So through the outcome of World War I the French in particular had got their revenge. And that was perhaps to be the nucleus of the unavoidable next conflict.

Sadly what went on in the salon railway carriage in the forest at Compiegne, where the case was settled, completely failed in placing the emphasis where it belonged. In 1914 it had been the German military under its commander-in-chief, Kaiser Wilhelm II, in the driver's seat, spoiling for war. Internationally, up to the end of hostilities in 1918 and the armistice, no German civilian government had been in any way involved. Then, as if by magic, the German military faded into the background, literally vanished, leaving a hastily scrambled civilian government, not really a duly elected one, to pick up the pieces and do what little damage-control remained possible. The German representatives suing for peace were all civilians.

In Germany the consequence of this was enormous. The German monarchists, rallying behind the military, were subsequently claiming that the 'democratic' government had stabbed the 'glorious military' in the back, depriving them of victory and honour. This was of course not true. It is a well established fact that at this point of the conflict the German armed forces were effectively finished and could not have gone on to continue, let alone win the war. The stab-in-the-back or *Dolchstoss*, in German, was an outright propaganda lie by those already having other plans and ideas. At some point along the way this was to play into the hands of Adolf Hitler, allowing him to stir up resentment, as was the highly strung political climate of the post-war turmoil.

The Fall

In July 1932 Germany's national parliament, the Reichstag, was due again for election. Despite a slight gradual improvement of economic conditions street violence had been on the increase. This took place primarily between the Communists and Hitler's NSDAP, in which the latter had the more effective propaganda and was more appealing, this in particular to a 'middle' of small to medium business and trades people, shopkeepers and farmers. The elections produced what was called a 'negative, anti-parliamentary' majority, meaning that no matter brought to parliamentary vote would be carried by a majority. NSDAP (37.3%) and KPD (14.3%) together received in excess of 52% of the seats in parliament and made clear from the outset that between them they were not agreed on anything. The monarchist DNVP at just under 6% were the third anti-parliamentary party, leaving only the socialist SPD (21.6%), the Zentrum (12.4%) and a number of lesser parties of a more conservative persuasion (together about 6%) to form a minority in support of parliament of together about 40%.

The constitution of the Weimar Republic gave the president far reaching powers, in particular to appoint the country's chancellor, effectively the prime minister, with responsibility for running the country.

To be able to have any government at all, President Hindenburg, using his special powers, introduced government by *'Präsidialkabinet'*, i.e. appointed by the president. When Franz von Papen, the first appointee, failed to get a parliamentary majority, Hindenburg appointed Kurt von Schleicher, who was able to hang on for a while but then also had to throw in the towel. This brings us to the fateful date, already mentioned, that was to mark a point-of-no-return in German history: 30 January 1933.

From this moment onwards there no longer existed any stable majority of democratic parties supportive of the country's democratic orientation. President Hindenburg could no longer appoint a chancellor that would command a majority in the Reichstag. In view of the sweeping powers that the Weimar Constitution extended to the offices of both president and chancellor this may very well be seen as the foreboding of hard times to come. After his several unsatisfactory attempts at appointing a chancellor that was likely to calm the situation, seemingly having run out of options, Hindenburg finally on 30 January 1933 appointed Hitler chancellor, a move that with the invaluable benefit of hindsight may well be labelled the beginning of the end. Hindenburg's rationale for appointing Hitler had been to forestall open rioting and unrest.

Now two men stood in the limelight: Count Paul von Hindenburg, duly elected president of the German Republic, and Adolf Hitler, leader of the National Socialist German Workers' Party, NSDAP, which held just over 30% of the seats in the *Reichstag*, the German parliament.

In World War I Count Paul von Hindenburg gained recognition as war hero for having defeated the Russians in the Battle of Tannenberg as commander of the eastern front, for which he was promoted to the rank of Field Marshall. Things went quiet for him for a while until he was elected German President in 1925, aged 77, widely acclaimed by the monarchists. In a democracy this may have seemed unusual, choosing him, an outspoken monarchist, but his conduct of the presidency was impeccable.

During his first term of office from 1925 onwards the country enjoyed a period of relative stability, ushered in by the devaluation of the currency, called 'Currency Reform of 1923', kindling Germany's hope of returning into the fold of internationally respected countries. Black Friday of 25 October 1929 with the collapse of the New York Stock Exchange pulled the rug from under the feet of those hoping for progress on the road to recovery. In an atmosphere of economic shock Hindenburg was elected into a second term of office. Elections for the Reichstag of 14 September 1930 reflected the change of mood in the country, producing a right-wing majority, with Hitler's NSDAP contributing 18.3% as coalition partner, bringing together mostly members of the disenchanted 'middle'. As international loans were called in the economy collapsed and by 1931 unemployment had exceeded five million.

In retrospect it is possible to identify those factors and circumstances that made it possible for Hitler to rise to power over a modern industrial nation in the heart of Europe. Leaving aside not directly related questions that concern Germany in a wider sense the focus is on those that really stood out as make-or-break issues for some sixty-six million people, to turn their backs on the prospect of living in a democracy in favour of embracing, implementing and supporting dictatorship. Hitler had already made it clear beyond the shadow of doubt what he had in mind, spelled out in his book *Mein Kampf*, My Battle, his political statement. He had written this during his spell inside military prison at Landsberg Fortress for his attempted coup to overthrow the government on 09 November 1923. The attitude of the German general public could be summarised by the following as being the decisive ones:

- There existed a lingering undercurrent of resentment, compounded by hurt pride, for having been treated unjustly by the victors of World War I, in particular by the harsh terms of the Treaty of Versailles, which had been intended to settle the conflict

- Wide-spread unemployment, reaching some 30% round about the year 1932 had fuelled an economic climate of frustration

- Memories of presumed 'good-old-times' made Hitler appear as the logical successor to the forever-gone, nostalgically glorified figure of emperor

This gave him cult status and elevated him to someone of a higher order, perhaps not quite 'God-given' but not far from it. But the great evil to outrank all other evil was ruthless and even violent Nazi propaganda that presented as enemies of the state Jews and any other groups of people not in line with the Nazis, as someone posing an immediate threat. In modern terminology: a clear and present danger, someone to fight in order to save the country, arousing a climate of fear, growing into hysteria and hate and offering material rewards for joining in the fight, mobilising the lowest known forms of human motivation: envy and greed.

To make sure the message reached the broad masses the Nazis had the SA, their uniformed storm-troopers, to show force in the streets and convey a superficially perceived sense of stability and order, albeit in fact order in the sense of Ordnung machen, bringing to heel those reluctant to go along, explained in an earlier chapter. Today we are very far from having anything by which to visualise the scenario. The closest I can come to it is to think of gangs of thugs, some kind of hell's angels look-alikes, uniformed as a new 'force of law and order', wreaking havoc and terror while pretending to 'be on the good side'.

At the time of being appointed chancellor Hitler was still an Austrian national, thus not even a German. Before the war that was to come he had volunteered for the German armed forces, the Reichswehr, performing certain intelligence-gathering duties. He was awarded the iron cross in 1918 and discharged with the rank of private in 1920.

On his road to the top he started at street level, in a manner of speaking, finding his way to the hotbeds of chauvinistic dissent of the middle-class common man, where he distinguished himself as a self-styled public speaker and met with friendly interest in many a vivid debate and at times heated dispute. He became a well-known figure in the circle of belligerent agitators that would articulate their anger, frustration and hate for the Weimar Republic, gathering regularly in the well frequented beer-cellars of Munich. He was socially isolated and had no recognisable education save for the rudiments of somewhat general, presumably private, studies of the arts and architecture.

Rather than trying to re-invent the wheel let me draw your attention to Ian Kershaw. Of the historians dealing with the phenomenon of Hitler he is perhaps the one to bring out the key points with compelling clarity. The following characterisation of Hitler is gleaned from his various publications, books and articles.

Hitler was a highly articulate demagogue, notorious gambler, ruthless double-crosser and clever tactician, devoid of any compassion or feeling of human warmth, with an uncanny ability to detect and turn in his favour many if not most of the complex undercurrents running through the country and shaping the mindsets of people. Above all he knew how the Germans tick and how to capitalise on that unique understanding.

Hitler had the talent to mobilise the masses. Before 1933 he played to those radically rejecting the Weimar Republic. He articulated their anger, frustration and hostility, offering the spectre of a brighter future. Hitler promised a better society, national renewal, the redress of humiliation and misery and the chance to get even with those that were to blame for the ruin of the country.

A competent negotiator, Hitler was able to reduce complex situations to their essential bare bones, instinctively homing in on the weak points of his opposite party. His ability at pretence could equally deceive high ranking diplomats as well as dignitaries of the

Church. His cynical negotiating skills reflected a combination of intimidation, bordering on outright threatening behaviour, sweet-talk and bland lies. He was obsessed by the mission to save Germany with no tolerance for opposing views. In sum he was able to represent the concept of national-socialism conclusively and with no room for debate.

In 1923 he decided the time was right for greater things and on 09 November 1923 he organised a hostile, armed march on the *Feldherrnhalle*, Hall of the Field Marshals, place of nostalgic reverence on Munich's Odeonsplatz, with the declared intention of bringing down the government. This attempt was instantly thwarted by the forces of order which opened fire and killed 21 of his comrades that were with him in the column. Hitler escaped for the moment but was apprehended shortly thereafter and sent to Landsberg Fortress, a military prison, on a five-year sentence but was released for good conduct after only nine months. The time in prison turned out to be a decisive event in his career in at least three ways:

- He found the time and place to sit down and write his book *Mein Kampf,* My Battle, which probably not many people read but which got him a lot of attention, in particular on the part of the monarchists, who suddenly discovered that he obviously brought certain qualities to the table that they hoped to turn in their favour and use for their own political aims.

- By taking a hard stand and risking his life he displayed bravery, which gained him acceptance by the military and would henceforth see him as being 'one of them' in spirit.

- But most decisively for him on a personal level was his realisation that rather than fight the system it would be more rewarding and a lot easier and safer to use its own weaknesses to his advantage.

On top of that the prison staff at Landsberg, officers and NCOs of the *Reichswehr,* treated him with great respect, even a degree of admiration, which turned the entire operation into a highly educational sabbatical, beneficial for him in culminating in the realisation that it was essential to play things by the book whilst capitalising on the book's weaknesses. We can assume that while sitting it out at Landsberg he will have closely studied all relevant rules and regulations, enabling him to emerge from his time-out with fresh ideas and a conclusive action plan. Above all he started making friends with well-connected people in finance and industry that were putting their feelers out towards him, offering more than moral support.

It is fair to assume that at Landsberg he will have developed and refined his policy and strategy, for once he got out he acted with the ruthless, blind confidence of someone who knows exactly what he is doing. Centuries of authoritarian rule had established a culture in which form was able to triumph over content. In other words: you could get away with murder, as long as you made it look right. And he was going to do just that.

Hitler latched on to that realisation and used it to his advantage in the furtherance of his ultimate goal: rule over Germany as a stepping stone to something even bigger. His ambitions at the outset had been national. But with increasing success they took on a life and dynamism of their own. When he had conquered the Benelux countries, France, parts of Scandinavia, Poland, Czechoslovakia and the Baltic States, Austria merged *back* into the Reich, Italy inescapably locked into an alliance, only England or Great Britain remained as the one European power left to challenge Germany's rule over Europe. When he tried to extend his reach into the Balkans and Soviet Russia he may have started seeing himself on the road to world domination, who knows.

Hitler had not wasted any time to extend and consolidate his domestic power base. The sweeping powers granted by the Weimar Constitution and a number of specific measures made the individual steps seem like little more than a walk in the park. Some of this is a repetition of points already stated but it is, nevertheless, impressive to see the various steps lined up as one compelling and rather dreadful chain of events:

- 28 February 1933, *Notverordnung zum Schutze von Volk und Staat*, Emergency Directive for the Protection of the State and the People, 'temporarily' (effectively indefinitely without a specific time limit) invokes a state-of-emergency that curtails or suspends a number of elementary basic rights and limits the sovereignty of the states; measure also carried by the monarchists

- 23 March 1933, *Gesetz zur Behebung der Not von Volk und Reich*, Empowerment Act, better known as *Ermächtigungsgesetz*, carried in the Reichstag by the prescribed majority for constitutional changes, collusion of the NSDAP and their monarchist coalition partners

- 02 May 1933, all labour unions are prohibited, their assets confiscated and leading members arrested and locked away

- 22 June 1933, decree to restrain the SPD Social Democratic Party, prohibiting any further activities

- 26 June 1933, decree for the confiscation of all assets of the Communist Party, *ex-post facto*; it was merely a formality to catch up on things already done

- 27 June 1933, the monarchist DNVP disbands 'voluntarily'

- 28 and 29 June 1933, the monarchist DDP and the DVP disband 'voluntarily'

- 5 July 1933 , the Catholic Zentrum party 'disbands voluntarily', pre-empting disbanding by decree

- 14 July 1933, *Gesetz gegen die Neubildung von Parteien*, Act Barring the Formation of New Parties, establishes the NSDAP as the only political party permitted in Germany

- 30 January 1934, *Gesetz über den Neuaufbau des Reichs*, Law to Restructure the Reich: state parliaments are dissolved; the sovereign rights of the states are transferred to the Reich; the government of the Reich is empowered to issue new constitutional law

- 14 February 1934, directives to replace the last remaining federal structures by the centrally organised *Führer-State*

- 02 August 1934, President Paul von Hindenburg dies and Hitler *de facto* assumes his powers in addition to those of chancellor

- 19 August 1934, Referendum to Merge the Offices of President and Chancellor, carried by a huge majority

By these measures Hitler was now firmly in the saddle and could devote his energies to consolidating his grip on power. From the outset there had been tension between the monarchists and Hitler's own personal power base, the SA, acronym for *Sturmabteilung*, storm troop, but only the acronym came to be used in daily life and official language alike. In conjunction with the various electoral campaigns, street violence and general agitation it had grown into the para-military arm of the NSDAP, which had some four million members. At its head stood Ernst Roehm, an 'old faithful' Hitlerassociate from early days. The success of the SA fuelled Roehm's ambition to reach for a more meaningful role in the country. Werner von Blomberg, a monarchist, was *Reichswehrminister*, head of the armed forces, the *Reichswehr*. Representing the position of the monarchists he insisted that the Reichswehr should be the only armed forces in the country.

- On 17 June 1934 former chancellor von Papen emphasised in a speech that the monarchists would not be 'squeezed out of the state'. Being an alert tactician Hitler sensed the danger-potential inherent in a disgruntled Reichswehr, even the risk of armed uprising against him and took swift and decisive action.

- On 30 June 1934 the top brass of the SA were lured into barracks and about a third of them assassinated in cold blood by Hitler's henchmen.

Among those killed was Hitler's predecessor as chancellor, General Kurt von Schleicher and of course Roehm, for whom Hitler had no further use. This event became known as *die Nacht der langen Messer*, the Night of the Long Knives. It served to take the tension out of the situation between Hitler and the Reichswehr and there was no future discord between them. Subsequently, once he had become commander-in-chief of the armed forces, Hitler set up his own, personal, armed unit, the SS, which came to be considered a top-elite fighting force and thus was not seen by the Reichswehr as competition. Being put in charge of all measures of security it became a powerful tool for the maintenance of Nazi domination.

Hitler's powers had become absolute and completely unchallenged. All strands of power converged in his hands. There was practically no hierarchy but an increasing bureaucracy and the prevalence of direct actions on Hitler's personal orders. The only way to topple the system would have been to topple Hitler himself. He enjoyed a state of reverence due to heroic, charismatic qualities ascribed to his person, which held on to the bitter end – for some people even beyond that.

Many knowledgeable people now concur that the actions leading up to World War II, the war itself, the way it grew more and more disastrous and the persecution of the Jewish people and all those in opposition, would not have happened without Hitler. But it I san undisputed fact that he did not act alone and could not have done all the things he did without significant support from others.

Even today it is not quite clear who really stood behind Hitler, facilitating those steps where you need a huge amount of help and of course money in order to progress further.

Can we be completely convinced that nothing of the sort will ever happen again in and around Germany?

As I said earlier, I cannot see any likelihood that Germany will start another war or persecuting groups of people. But we live in a different age with different challenges, possibilities and threats.

Let us hope the ghost-of-the-past is gone forever.

Enemies within – Post World War II Fallout

The Third Reich, the Nazi state, was defeated and surrendered unconditionally to the Allies, whose key players were the Americans, British, French and Soviet Russians. That was the starting point for today's Germany. Today it is generally recognised that failure to defuse the problem potential arising from the fallout of World War I led to the next global conflict, World War II. This prompts the question whether we have reached the end of the chain. Do we have adequate safeguards so as not to risk repeating mistakes? One of the major ambitions of the Nazis had been to gain more *Lebensraum*, living-space, for the Germans, as they called it. This is the result.

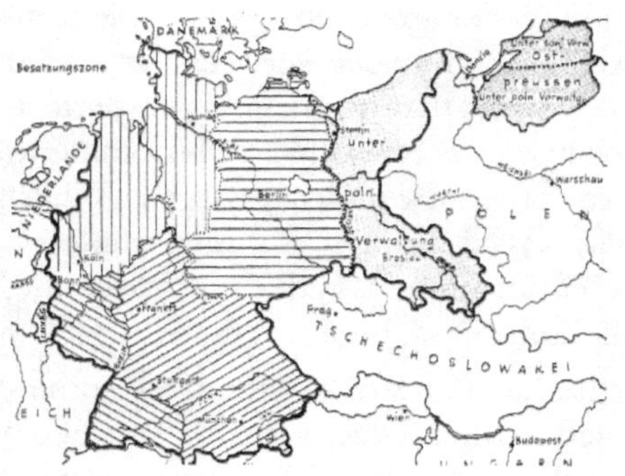

Legend
(counter clockwise starting at the top)
British Occupation Zone
French Occupation Zone
The Saar Territory, temporarily under French administration
US Occupation Zone
Soviet Occupation Zone
Annexed by Poland
Annexed by the Soviet Union

Germany at the End of World War II
Source: Kurz M. Jung; "Weltgeschichte in einem Griff"

The German provinces of Pomerania, Silesia, West Prussia and the southern part of East Prussia were annexed by Poland as repara4tions for war damages and the northern part of East Prussia by the Soviet Union; that meant all German territories east of the rivers Oder and Neisse. The remainder of the country was divided into the three western occupation zones, the British, French and American Zones on the one hand and the Soviet Zone, the latter primarily situated between the rivers Elbe and Oder-Neisse. Former capital Berlin was given four-power status under the authority of the four victors and the German province of Saarland was annexed by France but returned again to Germany at a later date. That outcome should be preserved in human memory as a reminder of what happens to a country that starts an unprovoked war of aggression with the intent of expanding its territory: it can backfire.

The three western zones in due course became the Federal Republic of Germany, the Soviet Zone the German Democratic Republic, West and East Germany, respectively, by short designation.

When after the end of Hitler's Germany the victors helped Germany to a fresh start they may have endeavoured to do the right thing; but circumstances soon put all good intentions to a severe test. In the long run there were too many problems to address and too few Germans that had come through the Nazi period with a clean slate. Compromises had to be made, some of a lesser order, others potentially far reaching and significant. As it turned out it was next to impossible to set up from scratch an entirely unencumbered new administration.

A process of de-Nazification was defined, whereby people were assessed on their past record, be it in public service, the armed forces or civilian life. Everybody knew that it was far from perfect, but thought to be the lesser of two evils, the other evil meaning to do nothing, delaying the process of getting under way again. Whilst in some cases the odd Nazi was waved through, it meant wholesale acceptance in others of the entire administrative infrastructure, picking off only the odd alleged 'top-Nazi', here and there.

The outcome is that in the hierarchy of government administration things mostly remained as they were, save for 'cosmetic' changes. This applied in particular to the judicial system and to a lesser degree law enforcement. German courts today are not much different, in principle, from those of the period of the empire, save for a general updating. In other words: the spirit of post World War II legal culture is that of the empire, not that of a modern democracy. This point is widely unknown or does not receive attention. The Germans do not know the difference, not ever before having lived under a democratic system of law. For the foreigners it is of no importance as long as they stay out of trouble, out of German courts.

Good government requires a good and sound basis in order to function well. It matters how your country is organised. When Prussian Chancellor Bismarck engineered the German Empire that was proclaimed in 1871 he had to bring together as many as twenty-six autonomous legal entities: the four kingdoms of Prussia, Bavaria, Württemberg and Saxony, ten dukedoms, eight principalities, the three free cities of Hamburg, Bremen and Lübeck and the territory of Alsace-Lorraine. The risk of thereby creating a cumbersome government structure, resulting in fragmentation and incompetence of the political process, was balanced out by the fact that you now effectively had over-all and all-encompassing one-man-rule on all big issues: the authority of the emperor stood above all and everything and any significance of a federal system was limited to the paper on which the relevant clauses were written. The emperor had the powers to take the country to war and used them. The federal nature of the over-all structure of the country did not provide any constitutional safeguards.

On 31 March 1933 Hitler had effectively abolished any states' rights that may still have existed. Once again whatever constitutional safeguards there may have been inherent in a federated system proved ineffective.

Those drawing up the new German constitution of 1949 came up with an array of states, constituting what was to become the Federal Republic. Using their German names they were Baden-Württemberg, Bayern, Bremen, Hamburg, Hessen, Niedersachsen, Nordrhein-Westfalen, Rheinland-Pfalz, Saarland and Schleswig-Holstein, eleven in all with Berlin still under special administration by the allies of World War II.

At that time the German political landscape was a wide-open green field. Anything would have been possible. It was argued that a federal system provided particular safeguards in respect of protecting the integrity of the nation. But such an assumption would not have been borne out by the facts from history. The federal systems extant at the time, both in 1914 and 1933 respectively, were incapable of preventing disaster.

The structure of the new federal republic was completely arbitrary. It could have been anything and it could have been more inspired. It retained some of the old encumbrances without welcoming new opportunities, creating an assorted mix of 'dwarf' city-states - as they came to be called - and states of vastly varying size, population and economic weight. For this there existed very little compelling historic justification, if any - but it was done.

The premise was wrong. You do not safeguard a country by any particular system chosen from any number of alternative possible ones. The only safeguard that works is the *people* that stand up for their rights and defend their state, their culture and their freedom. If I were a cynic I would call the creation of the Bundesrepublik the *Roman revenge*, where Consul Quinctilius Varus gets even with the successors of those who beat his army in the Teutoburg Forest in the year 09 AD. The 61 fathers and four mothers of the Grundgesetz, the people who drew it up, may have been full of good intentions. Someone should have taken them aside to give them insights into what makes a democracy work: if you want Democracy you have to implant it in the heart and soul of the people. Perhaps the allies should have kept the reigns in their hands a little longer until they could be sure the ship was in safe channels. As the constitutional assembly drawing up the country's Basic Law was made up of 61 men and only four women the outcome was bound to be male-heavy.

German unification in 1990 provided an opportunity for a thorough review when former East Germany was blended into the Federal Republic by adding it as the new states of Berlin, Brandenburg, Mecklenburg-Vorpommern, Sachsen, Sachsen-Anhalt and Thüringen. The West German Grundgesetz specifically called for a constitutional review as and when Germany would be united again. As things happened this was reduced to giving the East Germans the choice to join or else. As the 'else' was unacceptable to the East Germans, having had to wait for so long, acceptance was their only option.

Whilst today the Germans may proudly pat themselves on the back for a job seemingly well done they should ask themselves, whether they lived up to their own fundamental piece of basic law, the Grundgesetz, or whether they should not perhaps have used the opportunity to review the entire process from top to bottom and with all its consequences. But as we know that did not happen, and a golden opportunity was lost.

The preamble to the Grundgesetz states:

Das gesamte Deutsche Volk bleibt aufgefordert, in freier Selbstbestimmung die Einheit und Freiheit Deutschlands zu vollenden.

Which is translated: all Germans in free self-determination continue to be required to complete (the process of establishing) German unity and freedom.

This is an unmistakable order that the concerns of the East Germans should be given due consideration. Alas, those in power stonewalled the issue and bulldozed through. The wrong in having failed to do what was required of them was realised by the few that cared – and shrugged off.

State, Federal and Presidential Elections in Germany 2011 to 2015

Source: compiled from Zicht & Cantow 2011 (State names German spelling)

2011	State	To elect:	Term
Feb	Hamburg	state	4 years
Mar	Sachsen-Anhalt	state	5 years
Mar	Baden-Württemberg	state	5 years
Mar	Rheinland-Pfalz	state	5 years
May	Bremen	state	4 years
Sep	Mecklenburg-Vorpommern	state	5 years
Sep	Berlin	state	5 years
2012			
May	Schleswig-Holstein	state	5 years
2013			
Jan/Feb.	Niedersachsen	state	5 years
Sep	all states	federal parliament	4 years
Sep	Bayern	state,	5 years
Dec	Hessen	state	5 years
2014			
spring	All states	European Parliament	5 years
autumn	Saarland	state	5 years
autumn	Sachsen	state	5 years
autumn	Thüringen	state	5 years
autumn	Brandenburg	state	5 years
2015			
spring	Hamburg	state	4 years
spring	Nordrhein-Westfalen	state	5 years
spring	Federal assembly	German president	5 years

On a territory that is not much bigger than California, one of 50 states of the United States under one federal Government, Germany today comprises 16 states, each endowed with some degree of sovereignty. In the US the president is elected for a four-year term of office and there are two parliamentary chambers: the Senate and the House of Representatives. Elections are synchronised for the whole country so that every four years the people elect the president, all members of the House (note mid-term elections for members of the House) and a portion of Senators. That ensures a good measure of continuity and stability as well as the democratic process of critical review.

The German system could not possibly be more different. The country's chief executive, the federal chancellor, equal in significance to the president of the United Sates, is elected by majority vote of the *Bundestag*, the German parliament, in principle for a four-year term of office or a different tenure, subject to whatever parliamentary majority exists at any given time. He may be toppled if majorities change.

The chancellor is elected by parliament, *not* by general vote, placing the political parties between the electorate and the chancellor. Save for rare exceptions state and federal elections *do not* run concurrently and terms of office of state officials vary from state to state. This has as consequence that part of the country is almost at all times in the run-up to an election, somewhere.

Practically all states have coalition governments, the composition of which may vary from state to state and the majorities in *Bundestag*, the federal parliament, and *Bundesrat*, the chamber of the states, may be different. This system fragments the parliamentary process, resulting in general political inactivity for some time in the run-up to an election and very often leads to a complete stalemate.

The Germans seem to be happy with this, which may be due to the fact that they do not know any better rather than by conviction. It is a miracle how much actually *does* get done. But it is hard to ignore that many people are frustrated by the prevailing political culture. This has increasingly led to calls for the introduction on a nationwide scale of the instrument of a public referendum or *plebiscite*. Bavaria allows this instrument for state matters. Many people view the German parliamentary process as inadequate. From one election to the next voter turn-out is on the decline. There is growing disenchantment with conditions. There exists an undercurrent of volatility, which is hard to fathom out.

Looking in from outside the country it is incomprehensible how a modern, mature nation can live with such an inadequate and highly inefficient electoral process without wanting to change and improve it. The least would be to make all state elections run concurrently and for the same term of office and above all elect the country's chief executive, the chancellor, by nationwide, general vote, to endow the office with proper authority and stability and keep it out of the at times obscure doings of party-tacticians. There exists some discontent with the political system but its strength and nature are next to impossible to assess.

The Germans have a known tendency 'to stick it out', even to the last minute. In the dying days of WWII the country held out to the very last moment and then collapsed catastrophically, rather than calling a halt in good time. That should be food for thought.

Never Again?

We cannot deal with the Germans without looking at their past, asking the question: can it happen again, the incredible, unbelievable Nazi horror, the Holocaust and World War II? Hardly any country has faced up to its past as sincerely and with as much dedication as Germany. And therein lies a problem. The Germans have become so obsessed with a subconsciously harboured sense of shame over what happened in the past that they seem paralysed when it comes to taking a hard stand facing current threats. Yet Democracy needs to be able to do just that, when it is indispensable to fight those with vigour and determination that want to use the rights and privileges it gives to topple it. In order to be safe and sound Democracy needs to be strong and steadfast.

Today's Germany is a country where everything works; if it does not the Germans will attend to it swiftly. People are friendly. The atmosphere in daily life and in the streets is relaxed, generally free from threats or harassment of any kind and it is a pleasant country to visit, going to great length to present itself in a favourable light. There is very little noticeable violence or street crime, if any. People are generally helpful. Superficially there exists little justification for criticism. I want to take it one step further and state categorically that the Germans themselves are happy with their country and its living conditions, save for the very few that are not.

And yet: in the previous sections and chapters I identified a number of shortcomings that apply specifically to Germany. They are inherent in injustice and deficiencies in a number of fields. Let me recap:

- We noted the Germans' inability to prioritise, demonstrated to their own detriment in conjunction with the Nazi state

- The country's failure to commit both state and citizen to the common good as evidenced by its absence in the country's constitution

- The state's failure to treat all citizens equally and evenly as is particularly apparent in education

158

- An unfair economic system that pampers big business and industry under the banner of economic necessity, thereby taking from the poor and giving to the rich

This may be at the bottom of growing discontent that is smouldering 'somewhere' in the country, not yet a major force but the core of something that can grow exponentially if 'times go bad'. The Germans are very slow to protest and tend to go along with even at times outrageous injustices. But when they explode it can be dramatic with serious consequences, as happened in 1918, resulting in the abolition of the empire, compounded by the events of 1933, resulting in the abolition of the fledgling democracy that had started to appear. Both times the basic structure of the state was shattered, no more and no less, leaving the field to adventurism.

This aspect is alarming. A general undertone of ancient feudal structures lingers in the wings, somewhere, ready to break through and take over. Today's Germans are a peaceful and honest bunch, dedicated to praiseworthy goals. But they don't have a collective memory on which they can fall back of the need to solidly and irrevocably embrace Democracy. Time since the last disaster has been too short.

How well is Germany equipped for effective crisis management? In World Wars I and II this was next to non-existent. The Germans barged ahead without suitable in-depth preparations. They had no convincing and compelling ideology worth speaking of. In WW I the principal objective was simply 'to make war'. In WW II it was to grab land, stave off their own bankruptcy by plundering the treasuries of their neighbours and enslaving citizens of other countries as free labour.

That may explain how they came to go to war without having so much as an inkling of the risks that this would entail and what the chances of their success would be. The German army did not even have sufficient fuel reserves for a comfortable one-way trip to Moscow, let alone engage in fighting along the way or having planned for a safe return to Germany at the end of it. The Stalingrad army had no winter equipment and above and beyond that the Germans dissipated their military power in such diverse and remote theatres as North Africa, Scandinavia, the Aegean hemisphere, France, Poland and the Soviet Union, starting a completely irrational conflict with the Americans and all this in addition to persecuting their own elites and decimating some of the most constructive elements in the stratum of German population.

The Germans acted highly irrationally. Did they learn their lesson? Have things improved? We saw rather embarrassing flops, symptoms that cast the shadow of doubt on Germany's ability to handle large projects. And yet the country continues to be a leading economic world power and one wonders: how they do it. Or is it perhaps German economy that is running ahead, pulling the country along with it? Are we looking at a 'tail-wagging-the-dog-scenario'? If that is the case, what magic force is there masterminding this?

The Germans are happily underwriting the debt of much of Europe at a time when their own debt already accumulated is huge. As we saw there exists no credible exit plan, whilst still increasing it at a brisk pace. German writer Kurt Tucholsky wrote that the (German) economy is based on the mistaken belief that someone taking out a loan actually intends to pay it back . . . ever. He may have been a few steps ahead of his time.

- Perhaps this should be the moment to remember that the country was practically bankrupt at the end of WW I

- Labouring on until the Inflation of 1922, wiping out much of the accumulated wealth of the common man and woman

- Writing off huge debts in the world economic crisis of 1929

- And then once again in the Currency Reform, the Währungsreform of 1949

How (the hell) do they manage to do this? This latter point serves as an example, how the Germans grasped the opportunity, decided to survive and succeed and bounced back: everybody was issued and started from scratch with – for most – no more and no less than DM40 (forty German marks), handed out to every man, woman and child, the *Kopfgeld*, per-capita-money, to set in motion the new economy. In today's purchasing power that would not even buy you a bottle of Chivas Regal, but the Germans were able to build the new Wirtschaftswunder from that. I find this most amazing. Others would simply have blown it and asked for more.

Much as I do not enjoy getting back to the subject of Nazi past and would like to see it over and done with, once and for all, we cannot ignore it, not just yet. There does exist a lingering Nazi threat. Irrespective of encouraging evidence to the contrary there exists a latently present undercurrent of neo-Nazi sentiment. This is not limited to any particular part of the population and runs through all strata of society. There are cases of right-wing led street violence and there have been terror-style threats and even murders to intimidate people. This threat is real, not hypothetical. There appears to be sufficient funding from undisclosed sources available for such sinister activities that, rather strangely, do not seem to receive a lot of attention from German authorities

Germany has an excellent police force, well trained, highly motivated and incorruptible. If over an extended period they failed to suspect Nazi terror this leads to the disturbing conclusion that they may be blind to things connected with Germany's past. Is this the tip of an iceberg? Is there more that we do not see? Have the Germans been alerted to take vigorous anti-Nazi action? To the best of my knowledge there exists no evidence that parts of the German government apparatus are leaning to the right. That could be good or bad news. If it is bad it is very bad, for it means that a certain right-wing inclination is endemic – people having it without realising or thinking about it, which fires through to their attitude and obstructs their clarity of vision when it comes to recognising right-wing activities.

In the run-up to the Third Reich the Nazis cunningly used the stratum of under-privileged, insufficiently educated younger people to recruit their SA-storm-troopers, which served to intimidate ordinary citizens and make them susceptible for the lures of 'protection' by a strong hand. As we know this worked to the detriment of Democracy and led to dictatorship. The eastern parts of Germany, former East Germany, are as yet not as well developed economically as the west of the country with fewer employment and career opportunities and, conversely, more unemployment, breeding grounds for anti-state activists.

This may be the point to bring up the parliamentary NSU enquiry, in which NSU stands for National Socialist Underground. Eleven committee members of the German Bundestag, representing a cross-section of all parties entrusted with that task, rendered a scathing, unanimous account of their findings. Having reviewed more than 8,000 files and interviewed some 90 witnesses, they noted a 'historic' failure, 'incompetence of the police in the various federal states involved' and 'a complete breakdown of the legal apparatus'. The attitude of police and judiciary had been 'amateurish' and 'prejudiced' and the work of the BKA, the German counter part to the American FBI, was referred to as having failed. I cannot recall ever having read or heard anything in Germany that was as genuinely condemning of political reality as that. You find all this on record in official documentation.

What had happened?

During the period from 2000 to 2011 three young Germans, Uwe Böhnhardt, Uwe Mundlos and Beate Zschäpe, referred to as 'Neo-Nazis', roamed the country undisturbed and seemingly with impunity, leaving in their wake two terrorist attacks with explosives, ten murders and a string of bank robberies. In 1998 police in Jena had discovered their bomb-making lab but the trio were able to slip away undetected and vanish from sight. On 09 September 2000 a Turkish florist was shot dead point-blank in the street in front of his shop, marking the first of short of a dozen such crimes. During the ensuing period up to 06 April 2006 nine murders were committed with the same weapon, all victims members of the well established and respected Turkish business community, save for one Greek merchant. The series reached a brutal climax with the murder on 04 November 2011 of police officer Michele Kiesewetter. On 08 November 2011 police found Böhnhardt and Mundlos dead in their caravan. On the same day, Zschäpe set fire to the trio's apartment at Zwickau, where police also found the murder weapon used in the series and that of police officer Kiesewetter. Zschäpe later surrendered to police authorities.

So much for the grim facts.

Up to the moment when the bodies of Böhnhardt and Mundlos were found in their caravan police did not have the remotest idea as to who was behind these crimes and any reason why. Although nine murders were committed with the same weapon police did not make the connection. Not once did they consider a right-wing neo-Nazi crime; seeking the murderers in the environment of the injured parties instead, inflicting great emotional hardship on them. To compound the irony the police had set up a task-force code-named 'Istanbul'.

The committee of MPs from the German federal parliament sat for 1½ years, painstakingly looking at every possible angle. They were both horrified and appalled by what they found, stating that the police were chasing 'ghosts', disregarding a multitude of clues. In due course they found that a nail-bomb attack in Cologne that injured 22, carried out in 2004, was also attributable to the trio, adding to their brutal record.

It also came to light that the trio had had numerous helpers, in particular one who got the murder weapon and one who supplied the gang with false IDs and other papers. However, despite all the overwhelming evidence as to the right-wing orientation of the crime series the committee saw no collusion between Nazis and state officials, just 'blindness' and 'incompetence'.

Of course it would have been improper for the committee to speculate. They had to limit their findings to what they could prove, supported by hard evidence. We are nevertheless free to do our own thinking and wonder whether the terror-trio weren't perhaps moving about 'like-fish-in-water', using words ascribed to late Chairman Mao Tse Dung or Vietnamese leader Ho-Chi-Minh on the subject of revolutionary or terrorist movements. We should perhaps assume - although we cannot prove it - that there exists an 'underground' of helpers with a fascist agenda, as their self-styled name suggests, facilitating terrorist activities against state and society in the widest sense. This should perhaps be the moment to remind ourselves that prior to the Nazi rise to power in and before 1933 this practice was widely used. We now know to what ultimate and bitter end. However, if one brings this up in Germany today people are quick to dismiss it as isolated and insignificant incidents that in no way reflect what is 'really going on' in the country.

Rather than accusing some of the police involved of being Nazi sympathisers we should perhaps take into account that their authoritarian mindset prevents many in the police force from seeing things coolly and in an unbiased way, making a distinction between being 'somewhat' authoritarian, as many people quite obviously are, and outright Nazi sympathisers. The Nazi background to the crimes never occurred to them as that 'simply could not have been'. The victims had all been part of groups outside the authoritarian middle or mainstream silent majority, as I would like to call them, and I leave you to draw your own conclusions.

Do I think this is cause for alarm?

Yes! Absolutely!

World War II reduced the size of Germany by about a third. That is a bit like America having lost Texas and California in one throw. Looking at the Baltic States, Poland and the Czech and Slovak Republics from their respective point of view the outcome of World War II must be seen as a godsend, whilst the Germans appear to have shrugged it off.

Many Nazi top dogs were apprehended at the end of World War II, taken into custody and some of them tried, convicted and executed for having committed crimes against humanity, save for those that escaped punishment as laid out in some detail in Appendix 4.

More often than not wars are started for personal gains of their instigators and to grab land to expand their own territory. The Nazis failed on both these counts, losing their lives and a great portion of the territory of their country. And yet again there appear to be people that are ready to get up and march, demonstrate in the streets and commit atrocious acts of terror, clamouring for more violence in the pursuit of nebulous and yet very inhumane objectives. Why would they do this? Do countries or rather their peoples have such short memories so as not to know how all that is bound to end?

A disturbing realisation arose out of the Adolf Eichmann Case. When the Americans sent journalist/philosopher Hannah Arendt to Israel to observe the trial of this presumed 'monster', people were at first taken aback when she described Eichmann as a dull, colourless and very ordinary person, having expected to see a savage monster of sorts. She came to the realisation that one of the particularly disturbing facts about the Nazis was their ability to carry out their atrocities by using a multitude of ordinary, average people who turned into monsters by becoming part of the Nazi apparatus and culture.

There exists an account by the revered Italian historian and scientist Vanucio Bandinelli, who during the time of World War II was the director of the art museum at Padua. In 1938 on the occasion of guiding Hitler together with Mussolini, touring a number of museums and cultural institutions in northern Italy, he gained a close insight into Hitler's private personality. He was appalled when he came to the realisation that Hitler in his words 'had the mentality and perspective of a shopkeeper or small time employee'. In the German original text it says *die Persönlichkeit: eines kleinen Angestellten.*

Elsewhere he described him as a subordinate personality, like a streetcar ticket collector.

A feature common to both Hitler and Mussolini was their quest for absolute power coupled with delusions of grandeur, in which their ambitions ran way ahead of their capabilities. It now challenges our beliefs to think that the Nazis could have caused such a big splash, being as common and vulgar as they were. Looked at in the cold light of day and with the benefit of hindsight this remains a complete mystery.

Trying to come to a conclusion I am in a quandary. There is no clear-cut verdict. Today's Germany and culture are a mixed bag of brilliance as well as some rather scary items. Germany gives every impression of working perfectly well - for the Germans. To me the great unknown is the question, how well the country will rise to the great challenges that lie ahead.

Reverting to modern mythology I am prompted to cite George Orwell's Big Brother: ignorance is strength. The public is left out in the cold, not knowing how good or bad it really is and hence has no reliable guidance. Herein lies the real and present danger. To me there remains a threat of 'explosive change'.

That may have been behind former Chancellor Helmut Schmidt's alarming remarks in a recent TV broadcast (Phoenix TV - Die Zeit - Wirtschaftsforum Monday 12 November 2012). He went as far as saying: *"Wir stehen am Vorabend der Möglichkeit einer Revolution in Europa* - we (are) stand(ing) on the eve of the possibility of a revolution in Europe." Short of saying that a revolution is imminent he nevertheless stated that the potential is now a clear and present possibility. He identified a distinct danger scenario. Whilst Germany confidently presents itself as a staunch and trusted friend and ally of the West, disruptive forces within put the country under stress, aiming at preparing the basis for civic unrest if not outright uproar. During his time as German chancellor Schmidt was highly respected and gained outright acceptance as a level-headed 'upright and straight thinker', as he was often labelled. Should this man have been going that far off the mark? Despite his age at past ninety Schmidt comes across as someone fully in charge and in control of his actions and what he says. I think the man is real and should be listened to but his words of caution mostly go unheeded, as they did in this particular case, German nationwide TV or not.

Meanwhile many in the country continue to relish in a complete state of denial, think they never had it so good and that this might as well go on forever. Many of my activities as an engineer had to do with nature and the laws to which it performs. We look for stability and durability with most if not all of the things we design and build. We look for solid foundations and keeping in balance the forces that act on whatever it is that we create. We look for equilibrium. There are perhaps two significant states of equilibrium, when something is founded on solid rock or safe and sound ground like - say - the pyramids of Gizeh or when it is in a sustained state of dynamic or fluid equilibrium, like the moon circling around the earth.

Applying these two examples to Germany I am more readily inclined to think of an iceberg, floating on the surface of the ocean or an aircraft in flight. The iceberg has a visible part that may convey a peaceful image of stability. But its stability is determined by the parts that we cannot see, leaving us to trust and hope that all will be fine. With the aircraft it is much simpler. Its stability in flight depends on its aerodynamic lift, which in turn is dependent on its forward motion, created by the thrust that propels it through the air. If for whatever reason that thrust drops below a certain minimum level the lift that keeps the aircraft flying becomes insufficient and it crashes to the ground. Looking at Germany's over all tumultuous past I find it hard to see a solid foundation. For its dynamic stability we have to hope that the forces that propel it forward will be sustainable and strong enough. There is a thought that comes to mind. Germany may be in the same boat with Alice in Wonderland when she was told:

'You have to run very fast to stay where you are'.

When I felt that I was unable to come to a clear-cut conclusion I suddenly had one of those rare split-second realisations. On German TV I watched a program called 'Control', showing the forces of Law-and-Order in action. Two government immigration agents, patrolling the Autobahn, had intercepted two cars, both heading away from Germany. In one sat a young foreign woman that was married to a German that was on a temporary job in Germany. In the other there were five foreign workers that had come to Germany with perfectly valid work permits for Germany and had been one day late returning due to car trouble. In both cases the only offense that I could see was the fact that they had come and been there legally and were one day late leaving. To my admittedly internationalised frame of mind these were minor, insignificant technicalities, nothing that could not have been settled with - say - a €5 fine on the grounds of an unimportant, harmless detail. Not so for the young German immigration agent. He saw a serious offense and went ahead to write up the various people for prosecution on the grounds of invalid documentation.

There it was! The Germans' inability to prioritise and the (seemingly slavish) preparedness to follow orders! That's how it works - they follow orders to the very letter and heart and soul do not come into it. When asked by a journalist whether he could not have looked the other way the immigration chap said that he had been required by law to book the people - no ifs and buts. The law is the law with no room for interpretation.

I realised that the authoritarian German system reduces people to robots - they are neither good nor bad- they simply have their heart and soul removed. That was it - that Hannah Arendt had not fully grasped from the Eichmann case and lay behind peoples' ability to act without heart and soul, for German perfectionism had successfully removed them from the people in their service.

What a sad and equally frightening conclusion . . . .

Appendix 1 - Maps

The German Empire of 1871 at the time of its proclamation was made up of a multitude of separate and in part independent and autonomous entities. The driving force behind the Empire was the Kingdom of Prussia, which over time had absorbed smaller units and had become the most significant part of the country.

Germany at the Time of the Proclamation of the Empire
Source Wikipedia

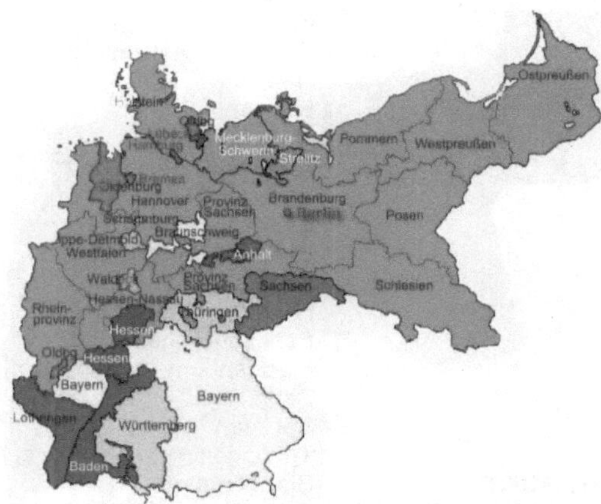

The German Empire 1871 – 1918
Source Wikipedia

This is the situation that presented itself after World War II. The victors agreed a line of demarcation with the Soviet Union that broadly followed the front as at the cessation of hostilities with minor corrections so as to better coincide with topographical or political criteria. Berlin became an enclave within the Soviet Occupation Zone and was itself divided into four sectors, one for each ally.

Germany at the End of World War II
Source: Map-Germany-1945.svg Wikimedia Commons

This is today's Germany, composed of 16 states.

The States
(German spelling)
Schleswig-Holstein
Hamburg
Bremen
Niedersachsen
Nordrhein-Westfalen
Rheinland-Pfalz
Saarland
Baden-Wurttemberg
Bayern
Hessen
Sachsen-Anhalt
Mecklenburg-Vorpommern
Berlin
Sachsen
Thüringen
Brandenburg

Germany after Unification in 1990 Source: Wikimedia

Appendix 2 - The Ups and Downs of German Economy

The Federal Republic of Germany speaks of itself as *Exportweltmeister*, meaning world champion of exporting countries. The underlying facts are well documented in the development of its GDP which in German is called *'Bruttoinlandsprodukt'*.

Development of German GDP – A Broad Brush Overview

Source: compiled from *Statistisches Bundesamt* – Federal German Office of Statistics

Decade/Year	Average Annual Growth of GDP	General Comments
1950-1960	8.2 % p.a.	The boom years of *Wirtschaftswunder*
1960-1970	4.4 % p.a.	The pace slackens
1967 -1968		1st recession; Labelled 'the end of the *Wirtschaftswunder'*, end of the economic-boom/reconstruction era; Chancellor Erhard, called Father of the *Wirtschaftswunder*, resigns; 1st 'Grand' CDU/CSU/SPD coalition political developments stagnate, then erupt into the 1968 student revolt
1970-1980	2.9 % p. a.	Moderate over-all average growth
1970-1973		1st 'oil crisis', delivery embargo by OPEC countries inflates oil price by factor of 4
1975	-0.9 %	Repercussions of the oil crisis become noticeable
1980-1991	2.6 % p.a.	Moderate over-all average growth
1980-1982	-0.4 % (1982)	2nd 'oil crisis'
1990		3rd 'oil price shock'; 1st gulf war; 'Internet-bubble' bursts - recession
1991-2001	1.7 % p. a.	Helmut Kohl CDU topples Helmut Schmidt SPD as German chancellor
1993	-0.8 %	Recession follows German unification
2001-2010	1.3 % p. a.	Moderate over-all average growth
2003	-0.2 %	Recession in Germany
2001 9/11		4th oil price 'boom'; recession in USA
2008 2ndqtr		Massive oil price increases; banking crisis in USA
2008-2009	-1.6 %	Massive recession during period
2009	4.7 %	Short recovery after the recession of 2008 towards pre-recession levels

Appendix 3 - Captain Coepenick

The Germans' Penchant for Officialdom

The shoemaker Friedrich Wilhelm Voigt (born 1849, died 1922) came to fame on 13 February 1906, when dressed up in a captain's uniform he held up the city hall of Coepenick, a hamlet near Berlin, arrested the mayor and 'confiscated' the city's petty-cash funds. Since age fourteen he had repeatedly spent time in jail on theft and robbery charges. In 1890 he got fifteen years for breaking into the cashbox, with a crow-bar, of the district court of Wongrowitz in the Prussian province of Posen. Most of his wrong-doings resulted from the fact that he was of no fixed abode, therefore had no identity papers and was unable to get a job and earn his living. In many ways he was a victim of circumstances, which primarily related back to the fact that Prussian bureaucracy tended to perpetuate an injustice, once it had been dealt on a person.

Because of his criminal record the Prussian authorities denied him residence status and the right to obtain a passport, at the time a prerequisite to getting a job. During his rather long spell in jail for a relatively minor offence he planned the coup that would end his misery, once and for all. As soon as he got out of jail he bought a Prussian captain's uniform from a pawn-shop along with all the salient paraphernalia and symbols of office, so that he could impersonate a captain of the 1st Fusilier Guards. After changing at the men's room of the local railway station he intercepted a small troop of soldiers in the street that were on their way back to barracks from exercise and another one that had been coming in the opposite direction. He ordered them to accompany him on a mission 'of highest importance and on the highest orders', which went down unchallenged.

Telling 'his men' that due to the shortness of time he had been unable to obtain vehicles he had them board a local train for Coepenick. He gave each of the men one Mark 'for expenses', treated them to a beer and a snack-lunch and then marched them on to Coepenick city hall. There he inducted the local gendarmerie post in his little army and gave them orders to seal the building and see to it that public order was maintained. Nobody was to neither get in or out nor move about in the corridors. Citing the authority of His Majesty Emperor Wilhelm II he then arrested mayor Georg Langerhans and city counsellor Rosenkranz, confining them under guard to their offices and instructed city treasurer von Wiltburg to carry out an audit of the city's ready-cash, after having sent for additional funds from the city's postal savings account. The audit revealed the sum of Mark 3,557.45 and a discrepancy of Mark 1.67 which he squared from his own pocket.

He ordered von Wiltburg to put the money into bags and seal them, giving him a receipt, which he signed *von Malzahn H i 1ˢᵗ GR*, i.e. captain in the 1ˢᵗ Guards. Von Malzahn was actually the name of his last prison director. He then ordered Langerhans and von Wiltburg to be taken by cab to Berlin under military escort, after having promised not to make any attempt to escape nor communicate with the outside world. His last orders were to the post office, in those days also the telecommunications office, barring any telephone calls for another hour. He ordered the soldiers to hold position for another half our and then return to barracks. With that he went back to the railway station with the money bags, downed a beer in one swallow at the station bistro, then boarded the train for Berlin and vanished from sight.

This event became a bit of a public laugh and the idiom 'Coepenickiade' found its way into colloquial German, denoting a successful hoax on the government. Voigt was arrested ten days later on a tip from a former cellmate who had hoped for a handsome reward. In the ensuing court case he got a four-year sentence but was soon pardoned on personal orders from the emperor, who had thought that this whole episode was 'hilarious fun', showing how well his subjects respected governmental authority, somehow missing the point that the joke was really on him.

Abroad the coup got a lot of attention and was seen as 'a manifestation of Prussian-German militarism', prompting the correspondent of *The Illustrated London News* to write:

> *For years the Kaiser has been instilling into his people reverence for the omnipotence of militarism, of which the holiest symbol is the German uniform.*

Years later Hitler was to apply a lesson learned from this event: he put his followers into uniforms, endowing them with a semblance of governmental authority. They came to be known as SA-storm troopers, helping him to conquer the streets and give his endeavours a touch of legitimacy to impress the public and to create an undercurrent of the Nazis' dedication to the maintenance of law and order.

Bibliography for Captain Coepenick

The 'Coepenickiade', as it came to be called, received broad coverage in the media as well as in literature and the emerging film industry. Please note that the original spelling of Coepenick eventually gave way to Koepenick (Köpenick).

These are some of the more prominent and better known examples:

Deeken. Annette: Der Hauptmann von Köpenick, Stuttgart: Reclam, 2005

Grosse, Wilhelm: Comments on and background to: Der Hauptmann von Köpenick, the play by Carl Zuckmayer, C. Bange Verlag, Hollfeld 2012, ISBN 978-3-8044-1956-8

von Hippel, Robert: Der Hauptmann von Köpenick und die Aufenthaltsbeschränkungen bestrafter Personen. German Legal Chronicle - Deutsche Juristen-Zeitung,.1906

Jeck, Marc: On the Highest Orders, Not a German Fairy-tale, Auf allerhöchsten Befehl. Kein deutsches Märchen. Die Zeit No 42 of 12 October 2006

Loeschburg, Winfried: No Pomp and Circumstance, The Story of Captain Coepenick, Ohne Glanz und Gloria; Die Geschichte des Hauptmanns von Köpenick. Ullstein, 1998, ISBN 978-3-548-35768-7

Niedzwicki, Matthias: The Basic Right to Freedom of Movement; on the 100th anniversary of the Coepenickiade, Das Grundrecht auf Freizügigkeit nach Art. 11 GG –Beitrag zum 100.Jahrestag der Köpenickiade des Hauptmanns von Köpenick, Verwaltungsblätter für Baden-Württemberg 2006

Rosenau, Henning: Captain Coepenick, a Notorious Criminal? Der Hauptmann von Köpenick ein Hangtäter? – Legal Comments and on the play by Carl Zuckmayer, 2010

Sprink, Claus-Dieter: Follow Orders – Sure! From Shoemaker Friedrich Wilhelm Voigt to Being Captain Coepenick, Unterordnen – jewiss! Aber unter wat drunter?! Vom Schuster Friedrich Wilhelm Voigt zum Hauptmann von Köpenick. Catalogue to Exhibition at Coepenick City Hall on the 90th anniversary, Köpenick, 1996

Voigt, Wilhelm: How I Became Captain Coepenick, Wie ich Hauptmann von Köpenick wurde: mein Lebensbild. Successive publications 1909, 1931, 1986, 2006

Zuckmayer, Carl: Captain Coepenick, A German Fairy-tale, Der Hauptmann von Köpenick: Ein deutsches Märchen in drei Akten. Fischer ISBN 978-3-596-27002-2

Frieling, Wilhelm Ruprecht: Captain Coepenick, The True Story of Wilhelm Voigt, Der Hauptmann von Köpenick. Die wahre Geschichte des Wilhelm Voigt.

Appendix 4 - Key Personnel of the Third Reich

The Nazis set out to create *Das Tausendjährige Reich*, the *Thousand-Year-Empire*, and conquer tracts and tracts of land. As we can see from the maps in Section 1 their efforts not merely came to nothing but resulted in reducing the size of German territories by about a third, a touch of history's inherent justice.

The main protagonists of the Third Reich and its command structure did not fare much better, as the following overview shows. This section lists the key personnel and thereby principal war criminals of the Third Reich. Some of the people at the very top sought to escape justice by committing suicide, among them Hitler, Goering, Goebbels, Himmler and Hess. Some simply 'vanished' but a large number of them were apprehended and brought before the International Nuremberg War Crimes Tribunal as war criminals. They faced charges on the following four counts:

1. Conspiracy against world peace

2. Planning, initiating and carrying out of a war of aggression

3. Crimes against the convention on the conduct of war

4. Crimes against humanity

It is to the credit of the victors of World War II that they carefully and meticulously dealt with each individual. Thereby they established a record for posterity of how civilised people deal with such a horrendous situation, and each one of those brought to trial was assessed and judged individually.

They all met their fate. One is tempted to quote a line from the American mystery series 'Dragnet', broadcast widely in the 1950s and 60s:

'Crime does not pay.'

These were Germany's main war criminals, including those brought to trial at Nuremberg:

1933 to 1945 War Criminals

Source: Qwika/Wikipedia

These were Germany's main war criminals, including those brought to trial at Nuremberg:

Hitler, Adolf (1889–1945)
From 1921 Head of the NSDAP Nazi party, from 1933 *Reichskanzler*, German chancellor, from 1934 *Reichskanzler* and *Fuehrer;* suicide 30 April 1945

Bormann, Martin (1900–1945)
Head of the party chancellery of the NSDAP with rank of government minister
Sentenced to death in absentia; disappeared at the end of WW II

Dönitz, Karl, (1891 – 1980)
Career soldier, grand admiral of the German navy, from 1943 commander in chief; after Hitler's death on 02 May 1945 head of the provisional government of the *Reich*
Sentenced to 10 years, released 1956, died 1980

Frank, Hans (1900–1946)
From October 1939 Governor of the *Generalgouvernement* , occupied Bohemia and Moravia
Sentenced to death

Funk, Walter (1890 – 1960)
Journalist, economics minister of the *Reich*, from 1939 governor of the German *Reichsbank*
Sentenced to life imprisonment, released 1957 on account of illness, died 1960

Frick, Dr Wilhelm (1877 – 1946)
1924 - 33 NSDAP-member of the *Reichstag*; from 1928 onwards NSDAP party whip, 1933 - 43 Minister of the Interior, thereafter governor of occupied Bohemia and Moravia
Sentenced to death

Fritzsche, Hans (1900 - unknown)
Journalist; from May 1933 head of news and propaganda department of the Ministry of Propaganda, tried in lieu of Goebbels, who had committed suicide. Acquitted

Goebbels, Joseph (1897–1945)
From 1933 Minister for Propaganda; in April 1945 German chancellor for two days
Suicide April 1945

Goering, Hermann (1893–1946)
Prime minister of Prussia, minister of the interior, German minister of aviation, minister for forestry of the *Reich*, *Reichsjägermeister*, *Reichsmarschall*, created the GESTAPO Nazi secret police
Suicide 1946 while awaiting execution

Hess, Rudolf (1894–1987)
From 1933 to 1941 second in command of the *Fuehrer* within the party structure
Sentenced to life imprisonment, committed suicide 1987 while imprisoned at Berlin-Spandau War Criminals' Prison

Heydrich, Reinhard (1904–1942)
Head of *Reichssicherheitshauptamt*, state security agency (RSHA) and deputy governor for occupied Bohemia and Moravia
Assassinated by Czech underground activists 1942

Himmler, Heinrich (1900–1946)
From 1929 commanding officer, *Reichsführer*, of the SS and highest ranking officer in the German police
Suicide by poison during interrogation by British officers on 23 May 1945 at Luneburg

Jodl, Alfred (1890 – 1946)
Career soldier, chief of staff of the *Wehrmacht* and advisor to Hitler on strategic and operational matters
Sentenced to death

Kaltenbrunner, Dr Ernst (1903 – 1946)
Lawyer, *Reichssicherheitshauptamt* state security agency (RSHA) succeeding Heydrich, head of secret police
Sentenced to death

Keitel, Wilhelm (1882 – 1946)
Career soldier, from 1938 chief of staff of the *Wehrmacht*
Sentenced to death

Krupp von Bohlen und Halbach, Gustav (1870 – 1950)
Lawyer and diplomat, tried as being representative of German
heavy and armaments industry
Case shelved November 1945 due to serious traffic accident of his

von Neurath, Konstantin (1873 – 1956)
From 1908 career diplomat, March 1933 to 1941 governor of Bohemia and Moravia
Sentenced to 15 years, released 1954 on account of illness, died
1956

Ley, Dr. Robert (1890 – 1945)
Chemist, responsible for abolition in 1933 of the free labour unions
and the introduction of the *Deutsche Arbeitsfront* state controlled labour organisation
Suicide 26 October 1945 while inside Nuremberg Prison

von Ribbentrop, Joachim (1893–1946)
1938 to 1945 foreign minister
Sentenced to death

Roehm, Ernst (1887–1934)
Long-time head of the SA
Murdered 01 July 1934 inside Munich-Stadelheim Prison on Hitler's
orders by SS-killer squad during the 'SA-purge' (mass murders of
top SA members)

Rosenberg, Alfred (1893–1946)
Architect, chief ideologist of the NSDAP and editor of the *Völk-
ischen Beobachter* Nazhi propaganda journal, from 1941 minister for
occupied territories
Sentenced to death

von Papen, Franz (1879 – 1969)
Vice-chancellor in Hitler's first cabinet, later ambassador to Vienna
and Ankara
Acquitted

Raeder, Erich (1876 – 1960)
Career soldier, until 1943 commander in chief of the navy
Sentenced to life imprisonment, released 1955 due to illness, died
1960

Sauckel, Fritz (1894 – 1946)
Sea captain in the merchant navy, from 1942 Hitler's general executive for labour, responsible for pressing some eight million women and men into forced labour in practically all occupied areas of Europe
Sentenced to death

Schacht, Dr Horace Greely Hjalmar (1877 – 1970)
Banker, economics minister and governor of the *Reichsbank*,
Since 1944 imprisoned by Nazis at Flossenburg Concentraton Camp, Acquitted at Nuremberg, died 1970

von Schirach, Baldur (1907–1974)
Youth leader of the Reich, governor in Vienna
Sentenced to 20 years, released 1966, died 1974

Speer, Albert (1905–1981)
Architect, from 1937 general inspector of construction for Berlin, 1942 to 1945 minister for armaments and war industries
Sentenced to 20 years, released 1966, died 1981

Seyss-Inquart, Arthur (1892–1946)
Governor of Austria, then governor of the occupied Netherlands
Sentenced to death

Streicher, Julius (1885 – 1946)
Elementary school teacher, from 1925 *Gauleiter*, administrator, for Frankonia, responsible for anti-Jewish, racist journal *Der Stuermer*, *The Storm Trooper*
Sentenced to death

Appendix 5 - Bibliography and Key Sources

NB: Some of the book titles have been translated from German

Benz, Wolfgang - History of the Third Reich - Geschichte des Dritten Reiches, Munich 2000

Bracher, Karl Dietrich - Controversies in History, Fascism, Totalitarism, Democracy - Zeitgeschichtliche Kontroversen, Um Faschismus, Totalitarismus, Demokratie, Munich 1984

Broszat, Martin - Hitler's State - Der Staat Hitlers, Munich 2000

Burleigh, Michael - Global Overview of the Era of National Socialism - Die Zeit des Nationalsozialismus. Eine Gesamtdarstellung. Frankfurt/Main 2000

Enzensberger, Hans Magnus - Hammerstein oder der Eigensinn, Frankfurt am Main 2008. Analytical Document

Fest, Joachim - Hitler - Hitler. Frankfurt/Main 1973

Frei, Norbert - The Fuehrer-State. Nazi Rule 1933 – 1945 - Der Führerstaat, Nationalsozialistische Herrschaft 1933-1945, Munich 2001

Grube, Hans J – SOS Germany – Liebes Deutschland rette dich! BoD Libri 2008

Grube, Hans J – End Authoritarian Governance – Obrigkeitsstaat weg! press twenty-one 2011

Hehl, Ulrich von - Nazi Rule - Nationalsozialistische Herrschaft, Munich 2001

Herbst, Ludolf - Nazi Germany 1933 - 1945, The Unleashing of Violence, Racism and War - Das nationalsozialistische Deutschland 1933 bis 1945. Die Entfesselung der Gewalt. Rassismus und Krieg. Frankfurt/Main 1999

Hildebrand, Klaus –The Third Reich - Das Dritte Reich. Munich 2003

Hildebrand, Klaus - German Foreign Politics 1933 – 1945 - Deutsche Aussenpolitik 1933 - 1945. Kalkül oder Dogma? Stuttgart 1990

Jäckel, Eberhard - Hitler's Reign - Hitlers Herrschaft. Stuttgart 1988

Kershaw, Ian - Hitler 1889 – 1936 - Hitler. 1889 - 1936. Stuttgart 1998

Kershaw, Ian - Hitler 1936 – 1945 - Hitler. 1936 - 1945. Stuttgart 2000

Kershaw, Ian - The Nazi-State, An Overview of Controversies - Der NS-Staat. Geschichtsinterpretationen und Kontroversen im Überblick, Hamburg 1999

Lehnberger, Klaus, Journalist, Nürnberger Nachrichten

Recker, Marie-Luise - Foreign Politics of the Third Reich- Die Aussenpolitik des Dritten Reiches. Munich 1990

Schmidt, Helmut - Phoenix – Die Zeit –Wirtschaftsforum 2012

Tessmann, Dr Ruediger – German History Seen Through the Country's Literature - Die Geschichte der Deutschen im Spiegel ihrer Literatur, Albenga 2008

Wehler, Hans-Ulrich - History of German Society 1914 – 1949 - Deutsche Gesellschaftsgeschichte 1914 - 1949. Munich 2003

The Author

After about forty years of working in America, Europe and Africa, first as a consulting engineer and then in aviation, H John Grube decided that there were other sides to life, like sailing around the world and writing books. After many interesting and demanding projects he said good-bye to engineering and aviation and has since developed a keen interest in environmental issues, believing that our world is a place worth saving, as it is the only one we've got. As the father of three grown-up children he firmly believes that we owe a debt of care and diligence to posterity and tries to live up to that wherever possible.

He hails from the grater Baltic Region that comprised Estonia, Latvia, Lithuania and East Prussia, the same part of the world as Jacob Gershovitz and Israel Baline, better known as George Gershwin and Irving Berlin. He shares his birthplace Koenigsberg with philosopher Immanuel Kant and witnessed the dying days of Nazi Germany, leaving his native East Prussia in April 1945 across the Baltic Sea in the last ship to make it out of Pillau, the last remaining sea port in the Eastern Baltic Sea, then still in German hands, moments ahead of the advancing Red Army. He later came to attend high school in Santa Barbara, CA, USA, studied engineering in America, Germany and the Netherlands and spent the greater part of his working life in the United States, the United Kingdom and eastern and central Africa.

H John Grube press twenty-one is

Hans-Jochen Grube author and publisher
press twenty-one
Cologne/Koeln, Germany

H John Grube press twenty-one is

Hans-Jochen Grube author and publisher
press twenty-one
Cologne/Koeln, Germany

www.ingramcontent.com/pod-product-compliance
Lightning Source LLC
LaVergne TN
LVHW091458170726
843492LV00001B/240